THE TALENT REVOLUTION

LONGEVITY AND THE FUTURE OF WORK

THE TALENT Revolution

LONGEVITY AND THE FUTURE OF WORK

LISA TAYLOR AND FERN LEBO

UNIVERSITY OF TORONTO PRESS
Toronto Buffalo London

ISBN 978-1-4875-0082-5

Printed on acid-free, 100% post-consumer recycled paper with vegetable-based inks.

Library and Archives Canada Cataloguing in Publication

Title: The talent revolution : longevity and the future of work / Lisa Taylor
   and Fern Lebo
Names: Taylor, Lisa, 1974 June 12–, author. | Lebo, Fern, author.
Description: Includes bibliographical references and index.
Identifiers: Canadiana 20189065621 | ISBN 9781487500825 (hardcover)
Subjects: LCSH: Age and employment. | LCSH: Older people –
   Employment. | LCSH: Personnel management.| LCSH: Employment
   forecasting. | LCSH: Intergenerational relations. | LCSH: Organizational
   effectiveness.
Classification: LCC HD6279 .T39 2019 | DDC 331.3/98—dc23

Lightbulb icon: Victor/iStockphoto
Running icon: bubaone/iStockphoto

University of Toronto Press acknowledges the financial assistance to its
publishing program of the Canada Council for the Arts and the Ontario Arts
Council, an agency of the Government of Ontario.

Canada Council   Conseil des Arts
for the Arts   du Canada

ONTARIO ARTS COUNCIL
CONSEIL DES ARTS DE L'ONTARIO
an Ontario government agency
un organisme du gouvernement de l'Ontario

Funded by the   Financé par le
Government   gouvernement
of Canada   du Canada

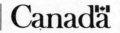

Canadä

FSC
www.fsc.org
MIX
Paper from
responsible sources
FSC® C016245

CONTENTS

PART THREE

CAPITALIZING ON THE INTERGENERATIONAL WORKFORCE

PREFACE

*We cannot solve our problems with the same level of thinking that
created them.*

– Albert Einstein

Before tweets and texts and clouds, even before "friend" was a verb,
baby boomers (those born between 1946 and 1964) outnumbered
everyone else in the workplace – and they were the drivers of com-
merce. They were the creators, the thinkers, the fixers, and the do-
ers. They were the entrepreneurs, the CEOs, and the presidents. But
what used to be isn't any more. Today, this same group of once-
energetic capitalists is often portrayed as showing up at work and
coasting. What's more, many managers seem to believe it's a kindness to let them do so. Some companies ignore boomers as a rich
talent resource and count on the millennials as the only people technically savvy enough to navigate today's technologically confounding workplace. But on close scrutiny, we identify boomers as
revolutionaries – a population of disruptors that is altering career
patterns, creating new expectations, and demanding inclusion. Indeed, this demographic is a revolutionary force – one of the five key
drivers shaping the future of work. And if, as a CEO, manager, or
HR professional, you want to improve productivity, fill the talent
pipeline, improve intergenerational effectiveness, and maximize
your competitive advantage, boomers are not to be overlooked.

The future of work is an important discussion as we come within
striking distance of 2020. Some look forward with anticipation to

the countless ways in which work will change over the next decades. Others fear a host of challenges triggered by an aging workforce, intergenerational dynamics, new working models, the need for a living wage, and, of course, artificial intelligence and automation. This book focuses primarily on the role that workplace demographics – radically altered by longevity – will play in the future of work discussion. It explains how longevity is the catalyst for the talent revolution, and how your organization can capitalize on the opportunity before it.

Every revolution has its own unique set of revolutionaries, trailblazers, casualties, circumstances, influences, and issues, and the talent revolution is no different. It is the logical consequence of a confluence of human realities and innovation that is transforming the world of work. It is nothing less than a major workplace upheaval in need of insightful leadership. *The Talent Revolution* illuminates what is happening in your workplace today and what is likely to occur as we look toward 2030 and the future of work.

One may well ask: What on earth is going on? Company loyalty has evaporated and the era of staying in the same job for twenty years has long passed. Indeed, it appears that workplace demographics have changed so dramatically that managing the multigenerational workforce is a nightmare. Older workers seem to clog the system and younger workers often quit soon after signing on. Companies are doing their best to urge out boomers while ingratiating themselves to millennials with games rooms, workout spaces, candy carts, and massages. The workplace is in flux and leaders are often at a loss.

What strategies must CEOs undertake to unlock the intergenerational potential within their workforces? What can managers do to supercharge the employees on the payroll? What can HR do to ensure an inclusive culture that motivates excellence at every stage and every age? How can the organization do what it does better, faster, cheaper, and more effectively than the competition? These are a few of the many questions we have been asking in our work with organizations big and small across North America. The book you are reading flows from what we have learned and the answers we have found. While not all our suggestions are universally applicable, the solutions we offer, the models we present, and the strategies we suggest have been battle-tested in the field, and they may provide the answers you seek. That's why we've written *The Talent Revolution* – to provide new insights and strategies for turning an aging workforce into a competitive advantage.

The topics of workplace change, shifting employment models, and labor strategy are hot, and they will undoubtedly trigger countless studies by a range of academics and corporate analysts, providing more than enough material to fill volumes for years to come. Our concern is more practical and immediate. As business practitioners focused on supercharging workforces and maximizing talent equity, we dig down and look more closely at the human element – now. Call us unorthodox, but we see demographics as the single greatest competitive opportunity on which smart organizations must capitalize. Furthermore, we suggest it demands urgent attention.

The workplace is a different arena than it was even a decade ago. Complicated times, complex technology, and thorny human issues have coalesced in recent years to create what often feels like a chaotic state of affairs, one that is as difficult to plan for as it is to characterize. But we see patterns in the chaos – patterns we have organized into a practical model so leaders can make sense of the dynamics now in play and effectively modify workforce strategies to capitalize on the changes they are experiencing.

We contend that the talent revolution is underway. Our work, our reading of the literature, and our own proprietary research and analysis leads us to this conclusion: the future of work is being shaped by technological and talent-driven innovation, and it can best be understood by examining five significant drivers – drivers that individually and collectively are transforming the way work gets done. We believe that the structures and cultural attitudes at play in most organizations are outdated and counterproductive, that they fail to take advantage of the intellectual capital currently within their ranks, that organizations can thrive with new thinking, innovative strategies, and new models, and that an attitudinal and structural reset will propel early adopters of the new models ahead of their competition. We believe this because it is already happening with our clients.

This book spotlights the revolutionary impact the changing workforce is having on today's corporations. We apply our research, findings, and recommendations to target those who must work together to navigate the shifting world of work in the context of business survival, growth, and future relevance: the CEO, concerned with new labor structures, markets, and conditions, and how these factors will accelerate or impede business strategy; HR leaders, who find themselves on the cutting edge of massive change that falls squarely within their area of responsibility; and frontline managers, who participate in career-focused, talent-related conversations with staff, often without a broader understanding of how the world of work is shifting.

We have divided the book into three parts, and we begin by making the case for joining the revolution. In part 1, we "zoom out" and offer a new model categorizing and clarifying today's workplace issues so that all three groups of leaders can take control of the revolutionary forces with which they must contend. We demonstrate that organizations have what we call a "Broken Talent Escalator®" – that is, career-path structures that ensure the boomer population either exits the workforce completely or stalls on the top step during their final decades of work. We assert that there is a generally unexplored stage of work after retirement age we call the "Legacy Career®"* phase. And we describe the problems with the status quo and illustrate how employers and employees are missing out on a

---

* The terms "Broken Talent Escalator" and "Legacy Career" are registered trademarks belonging to Challenge Factory Inc. All Rights Reserved.

significant opportunity to benefit from a currently undervalued work-life phase.

Part 2 addresses standard metrics and debunks the top five myths keeping companies mired in obsolete thinking, thereby hampering the development of a robust talent resource within their ranks:

- the myth of excessive salaries
- the myth of the best before date
- the myth of squandered budgets
- the myth of diminished productivity
- the myth of generational performance characteristics

While exposing the truth, we surface the underlying organizational needs that remain unmet and unacknowledged, the needs at the root of today's workforce dysfunction.

Part 3, the final section, provides actionable steps divided into segments, each applicable to a specific leadership role. It offers areas of focus and action for CEOs, HR leaders, and frontline managers, each of whom find themselves responding to different signs and symptoms of the talent revolution.

Throughout, we take an approach that advocates a deeper understanding and application of career development as a critical discipline that helps leaders tackle the challenges posed by talent management and career models. We provide stories, methods, and tools to improve performance, engagement, and intergenerational effectiveness, and we offer new plans for transforming traditional "retirement years" into a productive and meaningful work-life segment – a period during which the mature population within an organization achieves personal, organizational, and societal gains. And as we show, organizations will benefit from this transformation.

 As you read, you may encounter issues of pressing concern, issues you wish to tackle immediately. This graphic directs you to applicable solutions in part 3.

It is said that some people change their mind when they see the light, while others wait until they feel the heat. Our intention is to shine a burning light on the information you need to adjust your point of view and alter your expectations, thereby energizing your entire workforce and profiting from it. To that end, we present a new approach to understanding and managing the forces – the five drivers – at play in today's workplace.

A manufacturing company we have been working with found itself in a difficult position. With 55 percent of its employee base (and 67 percent of its leadership team) currently eligible for retirement, there was a growing realization that recent concentration on new-graduate recruitment would not address the significant knowledge and leadership gap this company would face. The succession crunch was not hard to predict. Based on the average age employees at this particular firm typically retire, as well as an understanding of the incentives built into the pension program, our analysis determined that without a significant rethinking of the employee lifecycle, and lacking new ways to capture, retain, and translate knowledge, this company would hit a wall in 2022. The uncertain timing and impact of succession is expensive and damaging to workplace culture. Helping this company understand the Broken Talent Escalator and how alumni could save their organization time and money – two solutions identified in this book – enabled the company to avoid the costly and dangerous approach of "waiting out the clock."

In another sector, a financial services firm with more than 120 years of history and culture recognized that the future of their business required a complete rethinking of core relationships. Instead of being the provider of traditional financial products and services to a relatively stable customer base, as they had been throughout their history, this firm wanted to transform itself into a flexible provider of technology platforms and services that react to new market and technology conditions. Its goal was to become a technology firm focused on the financial services market. A major transformation of this kind is enormously challenging, and executives wondered if their older workers were up for the task ahead. It was immediately apparent to us that engagement among senior leaders of the organization was on the decline at precisely the time the company needed strong cultural leadership from the top. Moreover, myths and stereotypes about different generations abounded. It was therefore critical that in transforming their culture, leaders acknowledged boomers' lifelong role as revolutionaries. Furthermore, leaders needed a deeper understanding of what employees in their fifties, sixties, seventies, and beyond require in order to perform maximally and continue to be engaged. The situation required a shift in core relationships, an essential part of ensuring that the old guard, the boomers, understood the new goals and were enthusiastic about helping the brand – a brand to which they had committed decades of service – thrive in this new economy.

The dialogue with senior leaders continues to evolve, moving from curiosity about workforce data to testing new ideas for workforce engagement and integrating our solutions for improved intergenerational workforce effectiveness.

Until now, there has been no manual, no useful model, and no clear pathway forward. This changes everything. We call for champions of the talent revolution. Prepare to lead!

THE TALENT REVOLUTION

LONGEVITY AND THE FUTURE OF WORK

Part One

THE FUTURE OF WORK: THEORETICAL MODELS AND FRAMEWORKS

1

THE FUTURE OF WORK
AND THE TALENT REVOLUTION

Around the world, academics, think-tank pundits, consultants, and event planners are immersed in a plethora of topics related to the *future of work* – a construct that requires looking ahead to imagine how the world of work will change between now and 2030.

Still nascent, the future of work does not as yet have a single definition. But organizations from the International Labour Organization to the Kauffman Foundation, Deloitte to McKinsey, all agree that the critical foundation for discussions about the future of work involves analysis, research, and prescriptions, and a focus on how technology will change the nature of work. The World Economic Forum has launched the "Preparing for the future of work" project, which asserts that as "technology develops at an accelerated pace, cognitive abilities and tasks that were once thought to be reserved for humans are increasingly being carried out by machines, causing growing concern about the impact on jobs and the subsequent risks for government, business and people. In addition, globalization, demographics, climate change and geopolitical transformations are already making a significant impact on the work landscape" (World Economic Forum 2018b).

As technology, mobility, and relationships evolve, the future of work demands new organizational perspectives and competencies to create a more human workplace. Indeed, there are many dimensions to a shifting work landscape and a number of facets and subjects to explore in depth, but academic research in these areas is just beginning to come to light.

We examine the impact of workplace and career models on the future of work in chapters 2 and 3. But rather than focusing on technology, we concentrate on the human impact of a shifting landscape and the immediate opportunity an aging workforce brings to organizations grappling with the ways their own work will change in the coming decade.

Effective leaders know that strategic planning and the setting of realistic objectives in a vacuum is folly. Context is required. Analysis

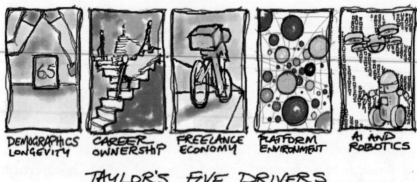

DEMOGRAPHICS LONGEVITY   CAREER OWNERSHIP   FREELANCE ECONOMY   PLATFORM ENVIRONMENT   AI AND ROBOTICS

TAYLOR'S FIVE DRIVERS

of the environment creates that context. The same is true of workforce planning. An analysis of opportunities, barriers, and influences yields the information you need to make informed decisions. This chapter examines the environment and offers a new model for understanding today's workplace turbulence, providing the context you need in dealing with the future of work.

The Five Future of Work Drivers and the Talent Revolution

Our experience and exploration in a wide variety of organizations has convinced us that both employers and employees are wrestling with the same five issues: demographics, career ownership, the freelance economy, the rise of platforms, and the impact of artificial intelligence and robotics. We have identified these as the major influences – the five key drivers – shaping the future of work. We call the model *Taylor's Five Drivers* and if, at first blush, the drivers feel amorphous, closer examination will reveal them to describe your workplace reality. They are the competing and commingling forces that fuel today's workplace turbulence and we will address their impact in the following chapters while maintaining our focus on the effects of longevity in reconfiguring today's workplace demographics.

Demographics and the Impact of Longevity

It is clear that all five drivers are not at the same stage of maturity, and it is important to note that right now we are in the throes of change directly associated with demographics, the first driver. Since 2011, when the first baby boomers turned sixty-five, older workers have become ubiquitous. Indeed, the impact of longevity on workforce demographics has created an unfamiliar workforce configuration, one setting new norms and expectations. Smart leaders will recognize the urgency of addressing the first driver while preparing for the impending disruptions fueled by the others. It is the first driver – demographics – that functions as a catalyst elevating HR, workforce planning, and career-related topics from functional to strategic, perhaps even vital.

Defining an "Older Worker"

Among academics, there is great debate about the definition of an "older worker." Some choose ages set out in legislation that regulates pensions and benefits. Others take a life-stage approach that acknowledges that actual numeric age is less important than the psychosocial characteristics indicating the beginning of a new phase of life. In our work, a life-stage approach has proven to be more useful than suggesting action based on chronological age – making it difficult to use "older worker" as an inclusive term. Some fifty-five-year-old employees may well have shifted into this new life phase while there may be sixty-seven-year-olds who have not. Indeed, in a study conducted in Ireland across all sectors, it was found that the label was being applied starting with workers in their late forties. That study explored how executives might consider using indicators other than chronological age in organizational decision-making (McCarthy et al. 2014).

In our work, we often hear "lack of engagement" as the reason for sidelining older employees. There have been many studies on what engages workers of all ages but, as indicated by James, McKechnie, and Swanberg (2011), little research has been done on older workers specifically. These authors refer to previous examinations of reciprocity, where employer consideration begets employee consideration, leading to stronger performance, increased efficiency, and a focus on improved personal and business outcomes. Their study of 6,047 older workers within the retail sector focused on identifying

which employer actions had the greatest effect on driving this population of workers to exhibit discretionary action and commitment
beyond basic job requirements (James, McKechnie, and Swanberg
2011). Other studies of reciprocity and older-worker engagement
show that engagement does indeed decline between the ages of
forty-five and sixty as workers begin to feel that they have upheld
their end of the worker-employee bargain and that their employers
are, at best, becoming ambivalent about their (the employee's) future
contribution (Kite et al. 2005). Interestingly, James, McKechnie, and
Swanberg (2011) pointed to the reversal of this trend for workers
over the age of sixty, and they sought to identify which job conditions drove higher engagement among older workers.

Author and consultant Dan Pink tackles the "puzzle of motivation" in his TED talk and best-selling books. Pink asserts that motivation depends on three essential elements: autonomy, mastery, and
purpose. Interestingly, for the last forty years, behavioral scientists
have routinely demonstrated that intrinsic motivators are more productive than extrinsic ones. Pointing to the same conclusion in
slightly different language, the 2013 BlessingWhite research report
on employee engagement supports Pink's thesis. According to the
report, "when it comes to drivers of engagement, clarity on the organization's priorities, getting feedback, having opportunities to use
skills, and career development remain at the top of the list for a
majority of employees" (BlessingWhite 2013). In other words, money
is not a prime motivator.

We question why, if science knows this, business generally fails to
take notice. Moreover, it seems that organizations that *are* aware
often apply these findings to their younger employees only. We suggest that intrinsic motivators drive engagement at any and every
point on the work-life continuum. Indeed, the research shows that
when specific job conditions are present, the evidence does not support the common myths about older workers. In companies with a
culture of inclusion, older workers can be less costly than, as open to

training, and as highly motivated and productive as their younger counterparts – topics we will address in part 2.

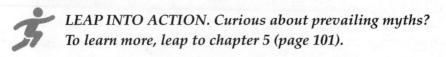

LEAP INTO ACTION. Curious about prevailing myths?
To learn more, leap to chapter 5 (page 101).

The business costs of misunderstanding or underestimating the impact of aging in the workplace has led us to focus primarily on the first driver of the future of work and to identify actionable strategies to deal with it. Our work in organizations across Canada and the United States indicates that while the other four drivers are playing a role in shaping the future of work, at this very moment longevity's effect on workplace demographics is producing profound impacts on the "now" of work, creating a need for organizations need to take immediate, urgent action in order to capitalize on the nature of today's intergenerational workforce.

Turning today's workforce demographics into a competitive advantage requires upending your point of view to focus on the far end of the spectrum. Millennials are neither your rescuers nor your tormentors. What's more, mature workers are far more likely to be technical wizards than generally assumed (Smith 2014). Old organizational charts are obsolete and intellectual capital already on the payroll is walking out the door. We believe it because we see the proof every day.

Demographics as a Competitive Advantage

We believe in challenging the status quo. We propose a new way of thinking that embraces the realities of today's working life and the demographic shift. Our experience demonstrates that with the appropriate attention and support, an attitudinal reset will overcome the dysfunction in our workplaces – so everybody wins. And while we challenge existing talent management and career models, we assert that there are underlying and unrecognized needs common to both organizations and managers. By addressing these common needs, new strategic thinking can prevail and clear, tactical action can be taken, turning your organization into a trailblazer in workforce transformation. As you broaden your view of work and aging, it is likely you will uncover unexpected opportunities to use a number of the tactics we suggest for exploiting the talent of a segment of the workforce that is currently underestimated and marginalized.

Organizations that recognize the interrelated impact of the five drivers shaping the future of work, and that take early, strategic action to capitalize on longevity, will be compelled to think about the relationship between employees and employers in new ways. Indeed, the employee life cycle itself is reconfigured as we reconsider the lifelong relationships that exist in today's highly networked world. Moreover, it is this shift in thinking about power, control, and the employment relationship that will enable organizations to capitalize on the (as yet unrealized) potential of a freelance economy in ways that do more than simply replace the old standard of full-time employment with a new expectation of precarious work. The shift in power and control is also where the talent and technological revolutions collide for maximum impact. In the United States, 81 percent of insurance executives indicated that by 2020 platform-based business models will be at the heart of their growth strategy. This prediction reflects more than just a simple shift in the employment relationship; it speaks to new lines of business, new markets, and altered relationships, where companies no longer offer either products or services, but flourish by providing a platform for the products and services of others – a change that has been described as the "uberfication" of industries, ushered in by the technological advancements of automation. An understanding of these platforms – which are still in their early stages – is a

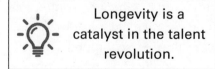

Longevity is a catalyst in the talent revolution.

critical part of predicting how AI and robotics will impact the jobs of the future.

The Technological Revolution Enabling Today's Talent Revolution

Discussions about the future of work often lead to an overwhelming number of topics, technologies, and tools, which are tossed around with little sense of clarity as regards hierarchy, impact, or logical action. Yet these questions swirl in a tornado of concerns. Will AI steal everyone's job? Do today's working arrangements doom all future workers to a reality in which insecure work is the norm? Will full-time employment fade into distant memory? We find that discussions often concentrate on how technology has changed the way work gets done with scant analysis of how humanity has been changing and reshaping the world of work in lockstep with technical advancements.

Prime architects and leaders of the technology revolution know that the human aspects of the way we live, work, relate, and create are important to the story of our own advancement. They acknowledge the relationship between technology and talent. Today's leaders, including Eric Schmidt, executive chairman of Alphabet, are being drawn into discussions about the ways in which technological advancement threatens employment and the financial well-being of the middle class. To paraphrase Schmidt's view, he believes that if we can create technologies that eliminate jobs, we can also create technologies that assist in the retraining of existing employees and the creation of new jobs (Future of Life Institute 2017). Professor Klaus Schwab, founder and executive chairman of the World Economic Forum, placed responsibility on individuals to prepare and navigate this technological revolution when he stated the following in 2015: "As new technologies make old jobs obsolete … every person will have to make sure they are equipped with the skills needed for this new era of 'talentism' – where human

imagination and innovation are the driving forces behind economies, as opposed to capital or natural resources" (World Economic
Forum 2018a). Much debate continues about who is responsible for,
and who is able and obligated to solve, the significant issues associated with the rapid evaporation of certain jobs – from retail cashiers
to drivers and beyond – as technology advances.

Technological change is a constant and continual evolution. Indeed, we see it as having become a "chronic" condition, important,
persistent, and perpetually in need of attention. In contrast, workforce change is often treated as an "acute" condition requiring urgent and immediate action to deal with a clearly defined episodic
event. However, both technological and workforce change are
chronic organizational conditions requiring ongoing management,
evaluation, and treatment (Taylor 2017).

A close look reveals that workforce shortages, new skill development, and uncertainty regarding the real impact of freelance labor
are merely examples of the drivers of the talent revolution shifting

DIAGNOSING ORGANIZATIONAL CHANGE

the world of work in ways that are as permanent and high-impact as the arrival of AI. Equally important, our experience convinces us that without a model to organize and explain what is happening in the talent revolution, each of these areas of concern is explored fleetingly and given attention only when an issue or event threatens business performance, after which it is pushed aside as interesting but not urgent. Or, equally dangerous, issues requiring a long-term, sustained focus are treated as if they are continually and permanently urgent, causing the organization to live in an extended period of acute stress. We find that our new model – Taylor's Five Drivers – provides a solid structure that enables corporate executive teams to tease out the difference between the symptoms and causes of workforce challenges, as well as offering a mechanism for identifying the order in which to tackle problems and discover hidden opportunities. We have used the model in manufacturing, financial services, professional service, engineering, and supply chain environments with strong adoption and relevance.

Key Points

- To make informed decisions about workforce planning, you need an analysis of opportunities, barriers, and influences.
- Results of academic research on the future of work is just beginning to unfold.
- Employers and employees are grappling with the same five issues: demographics, career ownership, the freelance economy, the rise of platforms, and the impact of AI and robotics.
- Taylor's Five Drivers is a model for identifying today's workplace dynamics.
- The impact of longevity on workforce demographics is setting new norms and expectations.
- Debate about the definition of an "older worker" continues.

- Research shows that when specific job conditions are present, the common myths about older workers are not supported by the evidence.
- Today's workforce demographics can be a competitive advantage.
- A shift in thinking about power, control, and the employment relationship will enable organizations to capitalize on new workforce demographics.
- New platforms must be understood to predict how AI and robotics will impact the jobs of the future.
- Technological and workforce change are chronic conditions requiring ongoing management, evaluation and treatment.

 LEAP INTO ACTION. Discover the five common myths holding organizations back by jumping to chapter 5 (page 101).

2

A SOCIAL REVOLUTIONARY LENS: WELCOME TO THE REVOLUTION

In this chapter, we begin by looking at revolution through a theoretical lens, then zero in on the talent revolution and your role in it.

Revolutions are sudden, radical, or complete changes that fundamentally alter the status quo. They challenge assumptions, models, expectations, and outcomes, presenting risks and offering opportunities for those who recognize the upheaval early and take leadership roles. While the concept of revolution is often understood in the context of violence, we use the term to refer instead to the pace and impact of a major, disruptive change. There are conflicting views and definitions of revolution as distinct from social change. Researchers in politics and sociology have identified criteria to indicate different types of revolutionary actions – criteria applicable to the talent revolution as well. Using author and researcher Ted Robert Gurr's criteria, for example, today's demographic-based workforce change can been identified as revolutionary because it satisfies five key dimensions: (1) it affects values, norms, behavior patterns, and situations; (2) change is occurring in these dimensions at the same time; (3) the impact is widespread, affecting all actors within the workplace; (4) there are patterns to the change that can be understood and predicted; and (5) it is happening right now and with increasing urgency (Gurr 1973). According to these dimensions, we can identify aspects of the revolution that are immediate and critical while also recognizing that these acute factors create long-term, chronic conditions that must be understood and addressed – the impact that lingers beyond immediate revolutionary moments. Examples of both acute needs and chronic, long-term impact will be explored in this chapter as we define and explore the talent revolution.

Since the Industrial Revolution spread to North America in the middle of the nineteenth century (1820–70), workplaces have been in a continuous state of change. But not all periods satisfy all five of Gurr's conditions for revolutionary change. Some changes are incremental and easy to integrate into the way we think about work and employment, while others are deviations of such significance that they are revolutionary in their impact, scale, scope, and challenge. In only a few generations, we have moved from an agrarian to an urban society, from decentralized to centralized work. We have replaced the value of artisans and their craftsmanship with an emphasis on automation and mass production. We have transformed from a marketplace of goods to an environment where almost everything is available as a service.

The shift to a service-based economy alone would have had a profound effect on the workforce. Furthermore, the rapid development of technologies that replace workers with machines, even within the services sector, leads many to wonder about the future of work as it relates to those who are less likely to have upgraded their skills over time, including the middle class and older workers. In his address to the Future of Life Institute, Professor Jeffrey Sachs demonstrates the profound impact technological advancement has had on the US middle class (Future of Life Institute, 2017). He notes that until the last hundred years, "work" has entailed hard labor, physical and continuous. He cites two specific trends relevant to our discussion that relate to the way work has changed over the last two centuries: (1) a reduction in manual labor, and (2) a reduction in work time (Future of Life Institute, 2017). What is striking about Sachs's approach to today's world of work is his assertion that the changes we are seeing today – be they technological or demographic – are part of long-standing patterns and changes made critical by rapid, recent advancements, but altogether new to economists and business leaders. The changes we are experiencing are important and chronic.

To assist in the understanding of today's talent revolution, we have integrated the dimensions of revolutionary change and applied them to what we see inside workplaces every day. We note that there are three key principles that help us translate the Industrial Revolution's historical details and workforce impact to illuminate the revolutionary changes with which leaders are wrestling in today's workplaces. These principles are:

Today's demographic change is part of a long, revolutionary cycle.

1 Workplaces have experienced revolution before.
2 Revolutions follow patterns, even when appearing to be disorganized.
3 Winners and losers emerge only when a steady state has been re-established.

Workplaces Have Experienced Revolution Before

Our discussions with human resource leaders across North America remind us that workplaces have been changing and reacting to revolutionary forces for hundreds of years. Yet, as demographics and employment models shift, challenging existing policies, procedures, relationships, and outcomes, leaders are convinced they are operating in uncharted territory, that their experience is unique, or that the challenges they confront have never before been seen. But there is a lot to learn from previous waves of workplace revolutions, and viewing the workforce in a historical context can ensure that today's leaders and their staff thrive in these revolutionary times.

As Schwab (2016) describes, the first wave of the Industrial Revolution is commonly associated with the introduction of technology and steam power, which transformed the production and transportation of goods and is sometimes characterized as a shift from "farm to factory" in an era that saw a decrease in the dependence on physical strength or prowess. The second wave is associated with the introduction of technology that enabled mass production and the mechanized assembly line. In both the first and second waves, the critical shift related to how and where goods could be produced. Both waves also resulted in a significant impact on labor due to cataclysmic business disruption and real job loss. Still, both generated new kinds of work because they unlocked new opportunities. Work shifted again, this time from factory to services. As well, new jobs replaced obsolete roles as workers moved from hand crafting to mass producing and distributing. Then, in the early twentieth century, women, too, began to participate more fully in wage labor, altering the composition of the workforce and challenging long-held attitudes about appropriate gender-based roles.

The third wave of the Industrial Revolution was also technology-based and equally disruptive, or perhaps even more so.

The third wave – often called the Technology or Technological Revolution – is marked by the introduction of supercomputing capability and the advancement of technology, with increasing value placed on knowledge (Schwab 2016).

According to Ryan Avent, author and news editor for the *Economist*, "a third great wave of invention and economic disruption, set off by advances in computing and information and communication technology (ICT) in the late 20th century, promises to deliver a similar mixture of social stress and economic transformation. It is driven by a handful of technologies – including machine intelligence, the ubiquitous web and advanced robotics – capable of delivering many remarkable innovations: unmanned vehicles; pilotless drones; machines that can instantly translate hundreds of languages; mobile technology that eliminates the distance between doctor and patient, teacher and student. Whether the digital revolution will bring mass job creation to make up for its mass job destruction remains to be seen" (The Economist 2014, 1).

World famous futurist and author Alvin Toffler categorizes the third wave of the Industrial Revolution as having a complete impact on our social, political, economic, and industrial structures. Just as cities replaced agrarian society, knowledge work has replaced physical labor (Toffler 1990). The changes to social and political structures are a result of shifts in where work is done, how it is done, and by whom, and these changes create new tensions as the way work is valued changes. Indeed, with widespread access to data and how we use it, what we know – our wisdom – becomes critical currency.

Observations from the Field

The Technology Revolution included the introduction of the Internet into everyday work and life. As a technology consultant in the mid-1990s, Taylor facilitated early-stage exploration discussions with companies that were contemplating use of the World Wide Web and the massive business implications this would entail. For some organizations adopting this new technology early was critical to their strategy and operations. Others resisted, often because there was still little proof that the Internet would actually generate its predicted transformative effects. What today seems like an obvious evolution in the world of work was not at all obvious at the time. Taylor predicts that by 2030, when the last of the baby boomers are over age sixty-five, careers that span well into people's seventies will have become just as commonplace as corporate websites.

This organizational change significantly impacted human resource departments and employees' career development. Canadian researcher Tom Zizys (2011) identifies a key organizational shift in the late 1980s, a time when companies moved from being integrated, with various functions and operations organized into separate but interdependent business units inside the company, to networked units with inside or third-party participants. In the

As the world of work changes, the pendulum swings and individuals gain or lose control over their careers.

new model, operational departments could just as likely be delivered by an external partner as by an in-house department. Ownership of labor shifted to outside the company walls and a new model emerged where everything – even physical production – could be delivered as a service.

Business historians and economists agree that we have now entered a fourth wave of the Industrial Revolution, one focused

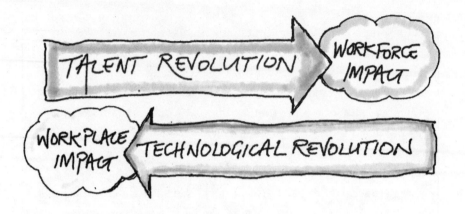

particularly on the impact of automation (Schwab 2016). As Schwab (2016) indicates, the revolution is just beginning, and it marks a fundamental change in the way we work and live. In describing the seismic impact of technologies still in their infancy on business, society, communities, and individuals, Schwab (2016) cautions us to pay attention to the size, speed, and scope of change. It is an unpredictable and volatile age best described as a talent revolution coinciding with the ongoing transformation of technology, and even a cursory examination reveals that massive shifts are underway.

Understanding revolutions can deliver an early competitive advantage.

As we enter the talent revolution, questions around who does what work, how that work is valued, and which models optimize both personal and corporate performance, are key to understanding how work, the workforce, and the workplace will evolve in the coming decade. And getting ahead in understanding what is about to unfold means harnessing a competitive edge from talent pools that may be invisible, hidden, or undervalued until the revolution is in full swing.

Patterns of Revolutions

In the 1960s, David Aberle presented a new model for thinking about social movements. In his work, he focused on the kinds of resources needed and how they should be mobilized in order for a social movement to fulfill its purpose. In his model, Aberle differentiated categories of movements based on the answer to two questions: (1) Who is changed? (2) By how much are they changed? The answers to those questions persuaded Aberle to call the social movements that resulted in radical change for everyone "Revolutionary Social Movements." While there has been some criticism of Aberle's model, especially its emphasis on resources as requirements for social movements, we believe it provides a useful lens for sharpening our view of what is happening in the world of work today. Aberle's categorization of social movements and change, like Gurr's determinants of revolutions, lead us to acknowledge that these are not ordinary times within the life cycle of the organizations we serve. In addition to the regular business cycle and market cycles, CEOs, HR leaders, and frontline managers are contending with a talent-based revolution. It is a lasting social change (Aberle 1966).

Since revolutions and movements follow patterns, we can extrapolate from previous revolutions and divine what to expect during the successive stages of the talent revolution. In our model, we have identified three stages that consistently occur before any revolutionary change takes hold and becomes fully transformative.

In the first or early phase, a good deal of attention is paid to a wide variety of experts and information sources. There's a lot of chatter, a lot of buzz and excitement. Data, opinion, research, and experience abound in fields that include technological advancement (the fuel for the different waves of the Industrial Revolution), social and political trends, and new thoughts, ideas, and models. At this stage, links or connections between these early thoughts and

concepts may be made, but they are tenuous, vague, or chaotic, since they have not yet aligned or coalesced. Instead, the many facets of the revolution operate as distinct areas for individuals and groups to explore.

 Early phases of revolutions are disorganized and chaotic.

As revolutionary forces gain strength and relevance, they begin to coalesce around common topic areas, and it is generally recognized that positive results are augmented when ideas, initiatives, or concepts are aligned.

Observations from the Field

In September 2016, Taylor was a facilitator at a day-long summit for senior HR leaders. Unlike other conferences, this event was entirely grass-roots driven. Like-minded chief human resource officers (CHROs) from a variety of companies formed their own group to discuss "the future of work." They complained that existing training programs and conferences lacked the strategic, future-focused agenda and discussions they craved, that topics were tactical, and that the focus was not at all revolutionary. Rather than turning to an industry association or consulting group, they banded together and created their own conference, complete with sponsors, keynote speakers, and a university setting.

Within a few short months, more than sixty peers joined them for a day structured around futuristic thinking, strategic skill development, community building, and design thinking. Without a deliberate intention to do so, they spent the day talking about the gap between the career challenges their staff was facing and the early experiments organizations might take to kick-start talent revolutions. As a group, they identified ground-breaking and game-changing actions HR could take to lead the strategic agenda in their organizations for the next few years.

Today, revolutionaries gather in strange and unexpected places – sometimes meeting through new technologies, sometimes not, but almost always reaching out in frustration and the hope of connecting with other innovators and visionaries.

Change is always difficult and it is rarely embraced without some influence that compels movement. So, even when ideas, trends, and advancements are aligned into common topic areas, widespread adoption of new revolutionary models and principles does not take hold until some sort of external catalyst forces change. At that moment, the promise of revolution moves out of the minds and hands of practitioners and into the mindset and awareness of the mainstream population.

As we consider what is happening in the workplace, we can't help but draw parallels to one particular catalyst that propelled the Technology Revolution forward. In 1999, attention and effort shifted dramatically to focus on preparations for the new millennium. Concerns related to Y2K caused almost everyone, even people with little interest in technology, to be consumed with questions about technology's impact on their daily lives. The fear was that the impending shift from 1999 to the year 2000 was going to impact everyone in radical ways. Barry Stanton of Emergency Management Australia, after having documented Australia's $12 billion emergency response preparations for Y2K, posed the question: "Was it worth it?" He concluded that the true value of the activities leading up to Y2K can be found in the lasting, permanent, and foundational shift that resulted in profound advancements in technology, preparedness, and interconnectivity (Stanton 2000).

In the intensive work we do with individuals and organizations, we see that innovation blossoms at the intersection of shifting workforce (employee/career) and workplace (talent management/career path) interests. Our observations are at both the micro level (focused on the experiences and stories of individual workers) and the macro or societal level (focused on shifting processes, stabilizers, and change). In understanding how these two levels might relate to each other, we find thought leader and author Michael Crozier's perspective on organizational analysis to be helpful. Crozier (1972) points out that sociologists have long extrapolated observations at the micro level to create patterns for understanding macro change. He criticizes this approach, explaining that the methods for understanding micro-sociological impacts are often not practical enough to allow for robust macro-level analysis. He calls for new ways of understanding how individual experiences of social change can be understood at the societal level, and he challenges sociologists to take a new look at the value of organizational analysis. Organizational analysis addresses the cultural aspects of what makes that grouping of people and processes unique. How do they collaborate? What effect do they have on each other? How does the individual impact the whole? And how does the whole change the individual?

Often, discussions about the changing world of work and, more specifically, shifting demographics, straddle different views that are specific to individuals and patterns that relate to companies, industries, or the economy as a whole. We contend that this shifting between micro- and macro-sociological analysis reveals that each of us is an actor in the revolution. Our analysis and recommendations sit at the intersection of the micro implications for individual workers and the macro changes shaping the future of work in our society, and we'll get to that. But first, let's look at how we arrived at where we are now.

Learning from Y2K as a Catalyst

In the third wave of the Industrial Revolution – the Technology Revolution – the impending crisis of Y2K served as the catalyst for significant change. Internet technology was certainly on the agenda of most organizations well before 1999, but technology's transformative and essential role was reinforced by the threat that business and personal activities would come to a dead stop when Y2K arrived at the stroke of midnight. Of course, by 1999 everyone – whether technophile or technophobe – was inseparable from their technology, and they were terrified that an interruption would be cataclysmic on a variety of levels. In fact, that New Year's Eve – the night that would usher in a new millennium – an astounding number of people across the Western world slept in their offices, ready to step in when necessary to avoid the anticipated disaster.

Today's catalyst is not technology-based; rather, it has to do with the reality of the first driver of the talent revolution: demographics now reconfigured by longevity. Increased life expectancy compels us to forever change our understanding of working-life expectancy. Longevity is the catalyst making demographics the most mature and predictable of the five drivers influencing the future of work, and for this reason we have chosen to focus on it.

For the last five years, Taylor and her team at Challenge Factory have spoken with HR and corporate leaders who have shared a common fear: that every baby boomer eligible for retirement will arrive at the office one day soon and hand in their notice – all on the same day. Companies tremble at the thought that they'll be left without a plan, without access to knowledge, and with significant gaps in key leadership and expert-class roles. In practical terms, the impending threat of mass retirement appears to be the issue that has ignited the talent revolution. But appearances aside, the talent revolution is much broader than the impact an aging workforce population will have between now and 2030, when the last boomer is over the age of sixty-five. It is a lasting social change that will force new career conversations, models, and methods of working. Longevity is the first of the five key drivers, and it is already transforming your organizations. Yet, as a catalyst it is often overlooked, misunderstood, or believed to be a short-term phenomenon.

Of course, we know the same-day mass-retirement scenario is unlikely to occur. But as a catalyst for change, it doesn't much matter if it actually happens or not, and the concern is very real within many organizations. Recently, one CHRO reported that his recruitment team was taking up to five times longer than usual to find new staff to fill the over five hundred vacancies they were expecting this year. Another vice-president asked Taylor to help them explore hiring veterans who may have retired from military service as young as thirty-three, to fill significant impending mid-career leadership gaps. Learning from our experiences with Y2K, most people – especially those who were not from inner technology circles – would describe 1 January 2000 as a "non-event" because the worse-case scenario did not materialize when the clock struck midnight. However, the fact that a technologically driven disaster did not strike does not diminish the impact that day had on crystalizing technology's significance in and relevance to our working and personal lives.

Similarly, the more realistic and emerging patterns of retirement will not follow previously predicted models. Yet the threat of mass retirement is enough to raise the specter of mass retirement – followed by attention, concern, and action. Fear propels us into dealing with the talent revolution, where focus on the workforce becomes paramount. Still, fluidity is the norm as the evolution continues.

Assessing the Timing and Impact of Each Driver

In the winter of 2015 more than nine hundred Canadian and international career and talent professionals assembled at the Cannexus16 Conference, a national career-development conference held in Ottawa. These professionals and experts in career education, counseling, development, and employment represented communities from coast to coast to coast across Canada. In one of the sessions led by Taylor, attendees were asked to comment on what they felt were important aspects of the talent revolution. While dozens of themes were identified, career professionals and HR leaders consistently commented on the precarious nature of today's workforce structures, and they articulated great concern for the broader economic and social impacts of losing stabilizing programs such as benefits and reliable, stable work. At that time, much of the response was focused on the macro implications of change – the social processes and stabilizers that were being challenged.

Two years later, at the Cannexus18 Conference, Challenge Factory ran a three-day research study. Where the previous interaction was part of a session specifically focused on the talent revolution, this time a more holistic approach was taken. On-site artists captured participants' reactions, questions, ideas, and dreams about the future of work as they attended the three days of learning and networking sessions.

In the years since the 2016 conference, discussion about the future of work and the impact on careers had become more mainstream. And while macro-level policy and structural issues still emerged,

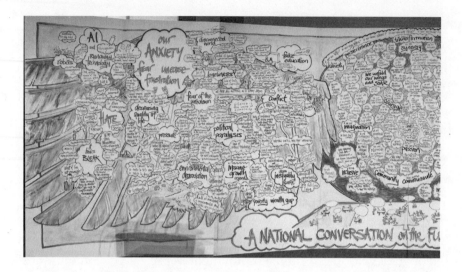

many participants at the 2018 conference expressed concerns for the more immediate micro impacts of the changing nature of work, including the significant shifts related to aging and longevity. In an on-site survey, 34 percent of participants indicated that demographic composition and longevity was the future of work driver with the most immediate impact (Challenge Factory and Creative Connection 2018).

Though the talent revolution is still in the emergent stages, significant shifts are beginning to occur. As Toffler (1990) reminds us, while living through emergent revolutionary change, life is turbulent. Everything we rely on for stability seems to be in flux. There is no steady ground as the economic, social, and political foundations of society shift. Revolutions challenge previously accepted norms and outcomes, and while a revolution presents a spectrum of risks, it also offers new and exciting opportunities for leaders who can envisage what lies ahead. But revolutions do follow patterns – and here is how the five drivers relate to each other in terms of their current level of maturity, impact, and integration into workforce-, talent-, and career-related strategies.

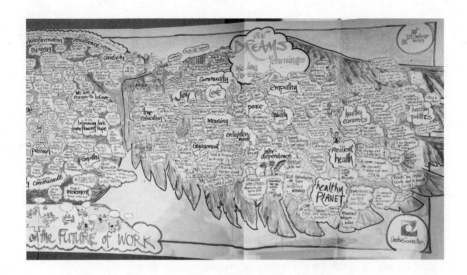

Not surprisingly, big decisions often spawn unintended consequences, and currently the unintended consequences of past workplace decisions are disrupting the equilibrium within organizations and, by extension, societies. For example, recognizing tenure instead of valuing work-product results has left some industries woefully out of date and unresponsive to today's market needs. Encouraging immigration without accepting foreign credentials has caused large populations to suffer from mal-employment, where individuals languish in jobs that are far below their skills,

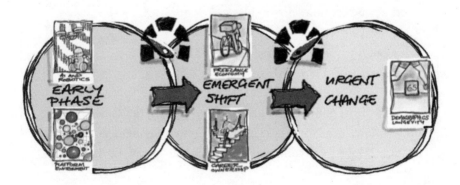

education, and capabilities. Setting and then removing a mandatory retirement age has created an undercurrent of discontent among younger workers who expected to improve their circumstances simply by moving into vacant positions that never materialized. There remains, in fact, an unspoken expectation of a specific time when people will or should leave the workforce. That expectation creates an unpleasant and costly undercurrent that, to the detriment of both the organization and the workers, marginalizes and undervalues an entire cohort within the workforce.

Observations from the Field

In February 2015 the Ontario government announced it was launching the Changing Workplaces Review (Mitchell and Murray 2016). A preliminary report issued in early 2016 shows that the purpose of this review was to consider what changes can and should be made in the context of Ontario's labor- and employment-law regime to continue to protect workers while supporting business in today's modern economy, with specific focus on the following workplace trends:

- the increase in nonstandard working relationships such as temporary jobs, involuntary part-time work, and self-employment
- the rising prominence of the service sector
- globalization and trade liberalization
- accelerating technological change
- greater workplace diversity

At the heart of this investigation is recognition of the need to understand the legal and policy implications of today's workplace changes. The review committee posed sixteen questions that asked citizens to consider what changes they are personally experiencing in their work and how current laws either assist in navigating these changes or appear to be outdated given today's experiences (Mitchell and Murray 2016).

We were particularly pleased to observe that the government's Changing Workplaces Review Committee intended to gain a deeper and more holistic understanding of the desired, potential, and unintended consequences of change in labor and workplace legislation. But while the final report describes projected workforce challenges and presents dozens of recommendations, we were underwhelmed by how the topic of longevity was addressed. In the 2017 report summary, the aging workforce is described as a burden on the system with no mention of the significant opportunities extra decades of productivity presents. In the words of the report, "as larger portions of the workforce will be older, there will be higher age-related costs such as pensions and health-related benefits as well as difficulties in retraining older workers for new jobs if the old jobs become obsolete. Many older workers who retire will later return to the labour force to non-standard jobs" (Mitchell and Murray 2016, 37).

We find that these conclusions reinforce common myths about the aging workforce. Moreover, they miss the opportunity to incorporate new life-stage models and ignore the impact longevity has on the potential productive contribution for workers of all ages.

Workplaces undergo continual change. Today's workforce has been dramatically altered by the shifting demographics of the employees within it. Employees know the only constant is change and managers are routinely challenged to make things work in "the new normal," where systems, resources, and expectations are different than before. And while the new normal is in a constantly shifting state, talent sources are changing too. In order to discuss, comprehend, and capitalize on today's talent trends, we must first understand how technological change has impacted the world of work over the last century – an impact best described as a revolution.

The Fourth Wave of the Industrial Revolution

The fourth wave of the Industrial Revolution has begun, and it's a wave that will be marked by increasing technological capability (Schwab 2016). While attention is currently focused on millennials, whose facility with new technologies is legendary, we are convinced that the emphasis is on the wrong end of the spectrum. What's more, demographics is both the first driver of the talent revolution and the catalyst that has created the conditions for subsequent revolutionary waves – explaining what is driving workforce models, structures, expectations, social norms, and outcomes.

In this fourth wave of the Industrial Revolution, the ability of objects to autonomously collect, share, and adjust to data – what is increasingly called the "Internet of Things" – is cited as the major theme, and it is this Internet of Things that dismays so many who fear that it foreshadows the end of the workplace as we know it (Pettey 2015). But researchers at Oxford University tell us that people have always worried they would be replaced by technology, and that while technology may create great wealth, it also produces what Joseph Schumpeter called "creative destruction,"and with it, a number of undesirable and unwelcome disruptions (Frey and Osborne 2013). Think of all the jobs required to support every bit and byte of technological change we see. We can conclude that current technological advancements, even the projected Internet of Things, are not the end of work and the workplace, but simply milestones in today's talent revolution.

Like the three waves preceding it, the forth wave of the Industrial Revolution is the result of transformational technology. However, today's world of work is not simply undergoing technology-enabled change. There is another revolution occurring alongside our rapid and incredible technological advancements – and that revolution is human. This is the *talent revolution*. It's a revolution we would describe as the marked shift or change in labor, work, and employment, with an emphasis on who does the work and how that work contributes to the social and economic health of our society.

Career Canaries in the Talent Revolution Coal Mine

The Technology Revolution had its own early adopters and warning systems. Some prescient companies started moving their operations online years before online shopping actually became possible. Others launched dot com businesses in the late 1990s, challenging traditional players and markets. But even those who didn't yet recognize the impact that technology and the Internet would have on everything we do and on how we do it, even they came to be part of the revolution. Unfortunately, they became the casualties.

Everywhere you look it appears that what once was set in stone is no longer absolute. Careers used to start in one's twenties. Retirement happened in one's sixties. Since the 1970s, career paths within organizations have been restricted by the organization – with the organization in total control, providing the structure and expectations for reasonable next steps in one's career.

The revolution in the workforce has begun in earnest. It is also clear that current workplace demographics, shaped by an aging population, is the first of the five drivers to reach a stage of maturity, thereby impacting businesses in their pocketbooks. Still, the next two drivers – career ownership and the freelance economy – are quickly permeating organizations and requiring obliging new relationships between the employer and employee. Boomers struggling to find their fit within traditional talent structures are both an indication and a warning that something is wrong with current talent systems and processes, and that employees of all ages are or will be affected. We note an increase in articles in mainstream publications and career-coaching blogs calling on employers to engage millennials with renewed focus on career pathing. However, the research shows that we may in fact be moving toward a "post-career-path" era, where careers shift and change more rapidly than formalized, predetermined paths can predict, with dispute among researchers about whether emerging career patterns will flatten or continue to reinforce upward mobility through organizations as defining characteristics of success (Baruch 2004; Lyons et al. 2012).

Professor Sean Lyons indicates that the life-stage concept of careers, introduced by Donald Super in 1957, categorized the focus of activity at each stage of an individual's career, beginning with exploration and establishment. Lyons suggests that these phase-specific activities described by Super may no longer be valid (Lyons et al. 2012). Professor Suzanne Cook also challenges Super's original and preeminent model in the careers field, indicating that today's workplaces demonstrate the need to consider updating the model. In her work, she suggests that the original life-stage for employees aged sixty-five and older, previously called "disengagement," should be replaced with a new life stage called "redirection" (Cook 2013). Redirection characterizes a change in career path or a career shift that employees must be aware of in order to take control of their careers in later life. As career models, theories, and paths continue to evolve, employees in this new era require greater career competence in order to take more control over their own careers and, in doing so, to challenge traditional and outdated approaches to workforce planning and predictability.

Change is underway and already impacts employees of all generations. Yet so far, organizations have failed to recognize that, like all revolutions, the talent revolution will follow a predictable pattern. If organizations accepted the current, apparently chaotic behavior, needs, and expectations of their staff as simply a component of an existing revolution, they would quickly see that the best way to capitalize on workforce change is to launch their own complementary revolution. In other words, if individuals are now taking charge of their own careers, and if those careers are being revolutionized, it is well past the time for executives and leaders to react positively and ensure that favorable conditions exist or are established to engage and retain their staff.

Trends of the Talent Revolution

The current decade – 2010–20 – has been declared the talent decade for good reason (Deloitte Consulting LLP and Bersin by Deloitte 2014). Demographics, mingled with career ownership and technological advancement, are challenging workforce structures and driving this revolutionary cycle. We agree with historians and economists who assert that we have entered the fourth wave of the Industrial Revolution – a wave we are renaming the "talent revolution."

As the workplaces of the future continue to evolve, we identify a constellation of three major influences shaping the talent revolution. Each is a new phenomenon, the final outcomes of which are still unclear. Yet, together they fuel an enormous blaze and begin to explain why we see what we see. Moreover, they serve as a guide for strategic planning and workforce tactics that leverage the current demographic shift. They are:

- the pursuit of improved work-life balance at all ages
- new employer-employee relationships that create a need for older workers to establish greater career ownership
- the emergence of a new concept with implications for older workers: the freelance economy

Chasing Work-Life Balance

Corporate psychologists and academics have come to the conclusion that members of the boomer and millennial generations have several traits in common – including attitudes and workplace values – and that a more detailed analysis of generational composition and life-stage approaches is superior to assumptions about age-based value systems (Lyons and Kuron 2013). Surveys of these demographic groups reveal that both cohorts value work-life balance, and that both express a desire to be in control of when they work, how long they work, and for whom they work. For millennials, the determination to balance work and life interests comes at the beginning of their careers, possibly because they are reachable 24-7 and quite naturally manage their work activities and personal pursuits without much concern for formal structure.

On the other hand, boomers believe they have earned their way to an improved work-life balance, and since they value their personal time and non-work-related activities, they insist they want control of these domains now. Boomers tell us they feel that with increasing demands to care for aging parents while still helping their children and grandchildren, it's vital to protect time for themselves and their interests. We also observe that work-life balance is a common characteristic of those in the Legacy Career phase of life – that is, the career they choose to pursue *after* so-called retirement age.

Boomers and millennials may share a common lifestyle vision.

It is important to note that while they are on opposite ends of the age continuum, both boomers and millennials believe that the line between good work and a good life can blend, and that work satisfaction is best realized when you can be yourself, both at work and at home. The need to establish a clear separation between work time and place versus personal time and place is disappearing, or at the very least it is blurring. Clearly, the industrial models of work are evolving and, as a result, so are we.

Organizations can capitalize on these attitudinal changes first by recognizing their significance. Demographics, ageism, technology, the freelance economy, career ladders and models are all dynamics that are fluctuating simultaneously. They comprise a comprehensive and interdependent system in which each component affects the others. As we move into part 2 we'll look at the significant business risks organizations face when they overlook older workers in their attempts to address these other areas – demographics, ageism, technology, the freelance economy, career ladders and models – of strategic concern.

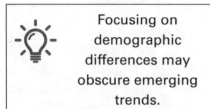

> Focusing on demographic differences may obscure emerging trends.

The Reemergence of Career Ownership

As the talent revolution progresses, relationships are changing. At this time, we see that individuals have taken some small steps toward thinking differently about the kind of relationship they have with their employers and the sort of career they want to build. Across the world, new models for engaging an over-fifty workforce is emerging as leaders from within this cohort find their own way through the corporate morass and share their personal experiences. The trend to take control of one's own career and to make choices outside the preferred options provided by organizations is happening with employees of all ages. We see it in the rise of "seniorpreneurship," with individuals over fifty setting out as entrepreneurs for the first time in their lives (Ozkal 2016). It's likely, in fact, that seniorpreneurship is a career path chosen in direct response to corporate ageism and the lack of Legacy Career talent structures within existing organizations. We see members of Generation X controlling their own careers too. We also see it with millennials, who may have heretofore unheard-of options such as sabbatical time, paid vacation expenses, and flexible work hours built into their contracts.

Traditionally, an individual's career was controlled or owned by the employer, but that is no longer true (Rahim, Golembiewski, and Mackenzie 2003). Today, the employee is in charge of his or her career whether they like it or not. The change in career ownership has a significant impact on the workplace revolution as workers recognize their personal responsibility in achieving their career goals and seek improved ways to achieve them. What's more, while millennials' willingness to leave organizations for new career paths demonstrates their commitment to managing their own careers, the shift in career ownership requires a completely new configuration for the worker-employer relationship. Interestingly, business leaders, researchers, and consultants readily accept the idea that the youngest employees are determined to defend their own interests, and organizations are racing to find new and attractive ways to establish an equal partnership with these newcomers to the workforce. But the same cannot be said of organizations' relationships with older workers who began their careers at a time when companies played a paternalistic role.

> The Technology Revolution has pushed the pendulum back so that, once again, individuals are controlling their own careers.

Millennials graduated into this environment, an environment in which the importance of self-actualization is integrated into workplace or career conversations and expectations. The trend toward career self-management can be traced in academic the literature to the late 1990s and early 2000s, when business schools began teaching students to think themselves as "Me Inc." (Jensen 1999). For decades now, students have been told that while they may work for an organization, they should own their own brand, know their own value, and manage their own careers. These classes were not available to boomers in their formative years, and most have not yet internalized the concept of Me Inc. – a construct that speaks directly to personal agency and self-actualization.

Whether the individual or the organization maintains career control is enormously significant because it establishes relationship patterns, norms, and expectations. It also defines the different levels and types of support employees expect from supervisors and managers. According to James, McKechnie, and Swanberg (2011), support from a supervisor is one of the key factors positively impacting employee engagement. When the employee is responsible for their own career, that employee benefits from a sense of autonomy and makes a personal commitment to pursue a path aligned with his or her own values and needs. Further, that employee expects supervisors and managers to inform, support, and expand next-career opportunities. Quite the opposite is true when the company is in the driver's seat. In such cases, there is a paternalistic relationship between employer and employee, with an assumption on the part of both the organization and the employee that both parties' values are aligned and that everyone's needs will be met, or that if they are not, the employee will accept an authoritarian attitude from the employer. Furthermore, supervisors and managers enforce, protect, and defend company-focused policy.

Currently, sixty-five remains the expected retirement age across North America. And yet the number of people continuing to work beyond that age is increasing despite a lack of organizational career paths, available work options, cultural norms, or a demonstrated interest by organizations in having these employees stay. This refusal to leave when all organizational cues and structures are designed to push them out shows that employees are asserting their wish for individual career management over corporate career interests. Yet many mature workers who come to work every day find themselves merely marching in place. Organizations have not shifted from traditional career-path models to models in synch with an extended working life, even while common indicators such as "engagement" suggest that the workforce is behaving differently than in the past.

Beyond the new dynamic of lengthened working lives, employees are actively indicating that the integration of work and life is an increasing concern. At the same time, the mainstream media associates innovative career approaches and self-directed career ownership with the way younger generations experience careers. But older workers are also expressing a desire for better work-life balance, ongoing learning and development, and meaningful or purposeful work. Lyons's Canadian studies show that while the boomer population is similar to other generations in terms of engagement factors, they are uniquely excluded and disconnected from career development as a mechanism for driving engagement. While today's employees have more control over their own careers than in previous decades – control that keeps increasing – boomers seem stuck. Accustomed to a lifetime of formal career paths that defined their next steps, they report a lack choices and a feeling of utter powerlessness. They sometimes complain of feeling invisible. It appears that in the main, the working-life path they are on has come to an end and there is no next step to take.

Challenge Factory conducted surveys of talent leaders within eighty-four Canadian organizations in 2009 and 2011. Based on our results, the deceleration of activity begins to creep in at around the age of forty-nine, when the quality of career discussions between employees and managers declines. In the 2011 survey, 26.5 percent of respondents indicated a preference for the filling of open positions from within. But, less than 18 percent indicated that employees over age fifty are offered training and encouraged to develop new skills in order to be able to change positions within the company. In 2003, Armstrong-Stassen and Templer examined training among older workers in Canada and found that fewer than 10 percent of organizations were engaged in such training (see Spokus 2008). In a more recent discussion of older-worker engagement, training, and career development, Cook and Rougette cite multiple studies demonstrating that employers do not consider older workers (defined as aged fifty-five or older in their work) suited for retraining. They also note that institutionalized ageism may be felt more intensely by older women, who face double discrimination: age and gender (Cook and Rougette 2017).

Discussions about work may continue as part of an employee's annual or quarterly performance-review process, but older employees report that this activity becomes focused more on completing the required interview form than on having a career conversation of any consequence. Indeed, 21 percent of the talent leaders surveyed believed this cohort was simply waiting for a severance package. Our findings suggest that since few managers know how to engage a fifty-three-year-old employee in a forward-facing career conversation, these discussions simply do not take place. On the other hand, the older employee may not realize that there are significant benefits to initiating such a discussion, and if it doesn't come up, they see no value in raising it. Moreover, should they actually raise the subject, most managers would

Training and development begins to decline long before retirement.

have no idea how to proceed. So, by the time employees are in their early sixties it is entirely possible they have not had a forward-focused career discussion with their manager for more than a decade.

At the same time that forward-looking career discussions seem to evaporate, the older employee may not yet have realized that the era of company control over career is coming to an end, or they may think that the emerging pattern of young people taking control of their own careers does not apply to them. As a result, neither the company nor the individual takes any action to move forward, and an entire cohort of talent is ignored while capable people mark time. That they become bored or disengaged is to be expected, and this is often attributed simply to aging. It is unlikely that organizations recognize the career potential of this cohort when boomers themselves don't appreciate it and believe they are still in a world where the company is in charge of their career.

> After a half-century of organizations defining their career paths, boomers can take greater control of their own next steps in today's more fluid environment.

Smart organizations will recognize that current career paths, relationships with employees, and talent-management systems are based on the assumption that by the time an employee has reached the age of fifty there can be little change to their career path or trajectory – an assumption that is counterproductive to a company's organizational and business goals. In fact, according to Willis Towers Watson, "40% of employees planning to work past 50 feel they are stuck in their jobs" (Willis Towers Watson 2016). Revamping current career-path options requires organizations to take notice of the large, vibrant, and productive workforce available to them among the population aged fifty and older and to find new ways to work with this cohort. Companies may be shocked to learn that if only they'd bother to ask, they might discover these workers may not want to continue doing what they have been doing for the last few decades. Equally important – perhaps even more so – organizations don't *need* these workers to remain stuck in the same role. Options must be available and offered – to everyone's benefit, as demonstrated in Munnell and Yanyuan's (2012) study of delayed retirement and the impact on unemployment rates of younger workers. As reported by the Economic Mobility Project, "Older workers' employment is positively related to employment of the young and prime-aged and has no statistical impact on unemployment or hours worked for either group" (2012, 2). All the evidence points to the same conclusion: there are new organizational needs demanding new relationships. New alternatives to traditional career paths that leave older workers stranded with nowhere to go must be identified. As well, individuals need to recognize that they have more control over their own careers than in the past. Smart organizations will make an attitudinal shift to take advantage of talent of all ages.

The Beginning of an Uncertain Era: The Freelance Economy

While some companies grow and multiply, and others divide or divest, still others shift in almost unrecognizable ways. At the same time that enormous changes are occurring in the employment sector, the definition of employment is changing too – morphing into what we now know as the freelance economy. Today, not everyone who works works for a company. Furthermore, not everyone who works for a company is a full-time employee of that company. This is the freelance economy, characterized by the increase in "non-standard working relationships" and sometimes described as shared work, flexible work, contract work, or contingency work. There's nothing new about contract, flexible, or part-time work, of course. What's new is the attitude or idea that this is a practical or even preferable way to actualize one's career in almost any field.

Recent reports indicate that the size and impact of the "gig" or freelance economy may be overestimated in mainstream media. The US government recently reported fewer independent contractors in 2017 than in 2005 (US Department of Labor 2017). At the Queen's International Institute on Social Policy in 2018, Taylor spoke with leaders of global "future of work" researchers from France, Germany, the United Kingdom, the United States, and Canada. All cautioned that despite media headlines to the contrary, in most OECD economies, data on the freelance labor force indicates that the number of freelancers is either stable or in slight decline. This finding may reflect how a "freelance worker" is defined. It is unclear whether or not freelance workers in nontraditional fields, such as Airbnb "innkeepers" or neighborhood dog walkers, include these activities as work when asked. At the time of this writing, we recognize there is more to learn about the pending impact of freelance employment structures. Still, we are not concerned with the relative size of the freelance workforce.

Employment relationships previously deemed inferior are becoming common and even preferred forms of association.

Rather, we focus on an unquestionably new attitude or idea – that the freelance economy is a practical or preferable way to actualize one's career goals.

It is important to separate hype from data related to the freelance economy. While some studies indicate that as much as 50 percent of working adults will join the freelance economy by 2020 (Rashid 2016), we are cautiously monitoring more conservative reports that focus less on the size of the workforce and instead demonstrate the shifting relationship between employers and employees. A new poll conducted by NPR and Marist Poll revealed that in America right now, 20 percent of jobs are held by contract workers (Marist Poll 2018). Indeed, in the very near future, it is likely that full-time workers will make up only a small minority of the workforce. And while the advantage to companies is clear – great financial savings in salaries, space requirements, and benefits – the rise of the freelance economy has produced some gargantuan wins for some individuals.

At the time of writing, it is clear that freelance models have begun to change the way both employers and employees think about their relationship and what might be possible. However, several troubling trends have also emerged in this initial, messy revolutionary stage. Both younger and older workers are experiencing extended periods of unemployment or underemployment. Among younger workers there are concerns about the length of time it takes for new graduates to find, secure, and thrive in full-time positions or their equivalent. Among older workers the emotional costs of unemployment and underemployment are high, and the longer it takes to find work, the more their age works against them and the less likely they are to find work (Bernard, 2012). Incidentally, in this new economy, the customary benefits granted full-time employees are absent, thus prompting the establishment of freelance unions – all in an effort to protect workers with few protections and increase bargaining power for workers with little power. In fact, the future power, potential, and impact of the freelance economy is not yet fully known. But its existence has drawn significant interest and concern, persuading us to include it as one of the five drivers.

Observations from the Field

In the immediate aftermath of the financial crash of 2008, two of Lebo's clients were unexpectedly and unceremoniously walked out the door of their respective financial institutions. Lebo had worked for each of these women over a period of several years, and she knew them to be highly respected by peers, employees, and the industry. Both were successful VPs in major multinational organizations who knew each other only as competitors. Both were stunned by the sudden turn of events.

Each woman had proven her metal in a predominantly male arena and neither had been out of work since the day they'd stepped into their first job, so they weren't terribly concerned about finding work. When Louise heard about Carol, she got in touch for mutual support.

At the time she was downsized, fifty-five-year-old Louise had been VP of business development for five years, a position that put her at the top of the food chain. At only fifty-two, Carol was a VP in another company, and she was routinely courted by headhunters.

When they were "let go" Louise and Carol each called on Lebo to help them update their résumés – documents Lebo found to be impressive professional histories packed with accomplishments and industry awards.

It's important to note that while the US financial industry is deregulated, Canada retains a number of checks and balances that kept financial institutions from imploding in the crash of 2008. The Canadian recovery was therefore much faster than the American one, and both VPs expected to find work quickly. But they did not.

They began to speak regularly and soon discovered that neither of their résumés provoked much interest. They couldn't be sure if this was a result of sexism or something else, but when they did get interviews they compared notes and found they'd been asked the kind of personal questions a younger applicant would never have confronted – disorienting questions, invasive questions, questions that might be considered on the edge, designed, perhaps, to surreptitiously reveal their age. For example, Louise was asked what year she'd been married. One interviewer laughingly compared her to his mother and slipped a reference to retirement into the interview. Carol dealt with much the same thing, plus she was asked on more than one occasion about the existence of grandchildren.

Feeling vulnerable and badly wanting jobs, neither candidate lodged a complaint, but these highly skilled, award-winning women were certain the issue was ageism. Nothing provable, perhaps, but palpable nonetheless.

They decided to take their years of experience off the page and off their LinkedIn profiles, and they began to get calls. In the end, it took Louise more than a year in an intensive job search before she found work. After nearly eighteen months, Carol accepted a VP position at a bank in a division that could make use of her skills; she was promoted within six months. Both remain with these organizations today, and both have won additional awards since coming on board.

Lack of security in one's work is widely recognized as a destabilizing factor at the individual level. It is also believed that when these destabilizing effects are experienced en masse, they can have undesirable societal impacts that are both destructive and difficult to reverse. According to former chief justice of the Supreme Court of Canada Brian Dickson, "A person's employment is an essential component of his or her sense of identity, self-worth and emotional wellbeing.

> Precarious employment arrangements are a symptom of the chaotic early stage of the talent revolution and the instability affects workers of all ages.

Accordingly the conditions in which a person works are highly significant in shaping the whole compendium of psychological, emotional and physical elements of a person's dignity and self-respect" (Dickson et al. 1987, 59–60).

While we agree with Dickson, we assert that, contrary to frequently expressed reservations, work need not follow a traditional model to provide stability and a sense of well-being.

The Freelance Economy and the Aging Workforce

A healthy income is not necessarily contingent on a full-time job structured in the way we have traditionally conceived of employment. We recognize that new modes and models of working are not equally accessible or applicable to workers in all geographies or industries. While we believe the trends we identify to be universal, our primary focus is workers in the skilled trades, knowledge sectors, and professions. Times have changed and services that didn't even exist a decade ago are essential instruments in a worker's toolbox today. Like a performer, the freelance carpenter, IT specialist, or professional writer may need an agent to do the job search, or a talent platform to make the job match. And a stream of part-time jobs or projects can produce an income far exceeding what a full-time employer is willing to pay.

As knowledge continues to gain strength as critical currency, it is not surprising that companies brokering expertise are growing too. Workplaces are becoming less about the equipment within their walls and more about leveraging the knowledge within their workers' heads. Each of us is connected to others more than ever before, and we have tools at our fingertips that ensure we can link, friend, like, and share what we know at warp speed.

A brand new industry focused on talent aggregation is emerging. Unlike staffing agencies of the past, today's talent providers offer individuals with knowledge and expertise direct connections through a highly nuanced technology – a talent platform – so job seekers can focus on what they know, rather than spending precious time building a business.

Observations from the Field

An increasing number of talent platforms are entering the marketplace. These platforms provide the infrastructure for people seeking a specific talent or skill. Because the platforms are technology-based, the match they make with an ideal candidate might result in a company in Saskatchewan having their graphic design done in Sweden, their office administration in Chicago, and their accounting in Newfoundland. Upwork is an early leader in this space, with hundreds of categories of skills that business can access to "get more done with freelancers." It's a sort of just-in-time service-delivery service.

While most of the early talent platforms do not segment contractors by age (a good sign that at least some of the world understands that people of all ages are players in today's freelance economy), a few new entrants are specifically targeting the capacity represented by the fifty-and-older workforce.

Kahuso is a Canadian-based talent platform that launched in late 2016. Its tagline – "Connecting Expertise with Opportunity" – reflects its use of a proprietary algorithm to match experienced candidates with talent-seeking companies for full-time, contract, advisory, and board opportunities.

A second example of platforms transforming the world of work in profound ways is the rise of new models of employee benefits and insurance. League is a Canadian organization in the emerging field of "insurtech." This platform, currently available to employees through their employers, provides employees with broad access to health and wellness services. The providers are not limited by category, service, or geography, and employees access and use the services they wish across providers and traditional insurers.

Employee health and wellness benefits are an increasingly important topic in the shifting world of work. The emergence of a cross-industry, provider-agnostic platform signals a future in which employees at all stages of their careers can be more self-directed when it comes to selecting the benefits and supports they want – as part of an employment relationship, such as League is set up to accommodate today, or as part of a broader marketplace in which independent actors can access the types of programs and services previously available only as a component of full-time work. This bodes well for older workers as they begin to consider what's next in their own careers: these individuals can now make decisions based on their interests, skills, and market demand, rather than being constrained by employer-focused benefits programs.

Today, entrepreneurial older workers are intuitively seeking support to assist in transitioning from a permanent employee who supplies labor to the provider of a service. This shift in the way older workers think about their relationship with employers is hard enough without having to encourage organizations to alter their thinking and recognize that there are new talent realities and opportunities on the horizon. Both the talent-supply and talent-demand sides of the equation are being revolutionized at the same time.

We urge you to accept the reality that the talent revolution has arrived. Right now, workplace demographics present you with a never-before-experienced workforce reconfiguration. And while you cannot opt out of participating in the revolution, the speed with which you respond to it is likely to be as important as the way you perform when adopting new technologies to supercharge your business.

Key Points

- Current workplace conditions satisfy Robert Gurr's criteria for revolution.
- Today's demographic change is part of a long, revolutionary cycle.
- Understanding predictable revolutionary patterns can deliver an early competitive advantage.
- Demographics is the first of the five drivers to reach sufficient maturity to impact businesses in their pocketbooks.
- Longevity compels us to change our understanding of working-life expectancy.
- The talent revolution is a lasting social change that will force new career conversations, models, and methods of working.
- Since individuals are taking charge of their own careers, leaders must react positively and ensure favorable conditions exist to engage and retain staff.
- Boomers and millennials have several traits in common.
- The importance of owning one's own career has reemerged; leaders will strategize to find ways for employees to assume more career control.

- Training and development begins to decline decades before retirement, with negative impacts on engagement.
- Employment is morphing to include what is now known as the freelance economy, with talent platforms acting as agents.
- Both talent supply and talent demand are being revolutionized.

 LEAP INTO ACTION. If you are a frontline manager or you support frontline managers, you will find action-focused recommendations and tools in chapter 12 (page 190).

3

A CAREER AND WORK LENS: BOOMERS AS REVOLUTIONARIES

Change is not the enemy; uncertainty is. And when you are dealing with a constellation of unknowns, estimates, hunches, and guesses, strategizing for combat can be confounding. In this chapter, we tackle today's workforce realities to assist you in amassing an effective arsenal.

We live in uncertain times. According to the experts in macroeconomics and the various mechanisms propelling the global business environment, we are experiencing a cultural upheaval of such depth and magnitude it is certain to revolutionize our lives and the way we work, play, and communicate (Schwab 2016). It is described as the forth wave of the Industrial Revolution, a tsunami driven by technology, fueled by global competition, and characterized by massive changes in the workplace, and it is "unlike anything humankind has experienced before" (Schwab 2016, 1). It is a paradigm shift felt around the world.

While the turbulence is palpable, less apparent is how to establish a profitable calm. By the time we gather the information we need and analyze it, the status quo has changed in a swirl of competing forces. Vague fears create an undercurrent of anxiety and it's impossible to know with certainty what lies beyond the horizon. Still, there are three things we know for sure:

1 Old workforce expectations are no longer reliable – many people's career arcs have changed.
2 Workplace ageism is insidious, rampant, and stifling.
3 We must adjust to new career realities to take advantage of untapped opportunities for growth and profit.

Let's address each of these realities one at a time.

Fact 1: Old Workforce Expectations Are No Longer Reliable

"Culture" refers to "the way we do things around here." It embodies our norms and expectations, and describes who we are. It informs our decisions, our strategies, tactics, and brand. It creates our present and defines our future – and it is the source of our mythology, for good or for bad. Today, even in award-winning organizations with praiseworthy cultures, age-based stereotypes and outdated career thinking has normalized the practice of writing off an entire generation of talent. It's possible that companies find it hard to establish workforce models, programs, and priorities that strike the right balance for employer and employee. This is either because there has been limited analysis, so decisions are based on outdated expectations, or because the analysis that exists is too granular.

When focus is limited to just a piece of the overall picture only, it is impossible to understand the whole. Context, content, and influences outside the field of vision may be completely overlooked. In this section, we "zoom out" and expose the dynamics of today's intergenerational workforce, review emerging lifelong career structures, and explore the impact of long-held ageist views that no longer serve society (Kanter 2011). Often, in times of change, the stories we tell shape the future. In this case, we have learned that the stories we tell may not accurately reflect the environment in which we live – that in times of revolutionary change, solid data matters. There may be many truths, but those that become the foundation for organizational strategy must be supported by sound evidence and a compelling narrative.

As companies struggle to regain their footing amidst a changing and seemingly unpredictable workforce, increasing numbers of young workers fail to find meaningful employment, and a collective voice shouts it's time for older workers to move on and make room for a younger, more talented generation – for the good of young workers, for the good of the country, for the good of the economy. Yet in fact, quite the opposite is true: trends in the workplace seem to contradict the call for older workers to retire.

From the *New York Times* we learn that close to a third of Americans aged sixty-five to sixty-nine are still working (Greenhouse 2014). The trend to employ older workers is evident in Canada too, where, for example, the Business Development Bank of Canada claims to be increasing its number of older employees every year. And there's more. IBM is recruiting retired people for special projects and nearly 20 percent of CVS Caremark employees are older workers (Sloan Centre for Aging and Work 2008). At Deere and Company, 35 percent of its American workforce is fifty or older. Deloitte obviously understands the value of older employees, because they've created a Senior Partner Program with the specific goal of retaining retiring partners. Equally impressive, for the fifth time ESW Incorporated made *Inc.* magazine's list of the fastest growing companies in America (Inc. 2015). These statistics do not support the view that older workers are clogging the system. We believe they are an indication that some forward-looking organizations have recognized new opportunities and are tapping into a rich and underused resource. Rather than viewing older workers as a cohort to tolerate until they eventually go away, these organizations have taken a new approach. The Society for Human Resource Management (SHRM) reports that 4 percent of organizations have a plan to retain older workers as a key part of their overall workforce strategy (Society for Human Resource Management 2015). What does this 4 percent know that other North American corporations have missed?

The numbers are no secret. Companies are fully aware of the increasing proportion of older workers within their ranks, and still, most are doing their best to offload them, completely oblivious to, or dubious about, the untapped source of wealth they are pushing out the door.

We need to "zoom out" to see patterns in the big picture and find useful answers to hard questions.

A focus on untapped existing talent may turn out to be the silver bullet companies need. Right now, both employers and employees are overlooking a significant opportunity to benefit from an undervalued phase of working life. It's time to re-evaluate current workforce models that assume that since a large number of older employees are on their way out, they should be excluded from career and talent opportunities. We have come to understand this view to be an indicator that organizations have what we call a Broken Talent Escalator, a structural and strategic discussion addressed in the next chapter.

Observations from the Field

In tackling this subject, we note the language used to identify older workers as a signal of negative feelings about them. Listen closely and you'll find such language unmistakably loaded with negative weight, thereby triggering negative perceptions. While merely grammatical comparatives, even the words "younger" and "older" carry emotional encumbrances. The word "younger" engenders thoughts of growth, development, and the future. "Older" connotes used up, finished, complete. Indeed, ageism is so deeply rooted in our culture and lexicon that finding a neutral or positive word for older workers is a challenge. Dictionaries list any number of synonyms for "older" – all of them value-laden. Whether it's "aged," "declining," "decrepit," "elderly," "fading," "hoary," "outdated," "senescent," "stale," or "senile," every descriptor conveys a degree of negative weight, except, perhaps, "mature," an adjective we like and will use frequently. And while there is no general agreement on when a person becomes old, being old or older is generally seen as a negative. In short, aging is understood to be a process of deterioration. It's no wonder corporate attention is focused on the young. Talk to CEOs, managers, and HR specialists, or eavesdrop on conversations at meetings, workshops, and conferences, and it's clear that we are quick to associate changes in today's workplace with the needs and impact of the latest generation to enter the workforce.

Fact 2: Career Competence Is Required

The field of career development is an underrepresented discipline in corporations. Since it is not necessarily part of formal human resources training, many of the tools and advancements in the field are unknown to corporate leaders. Career-development professionals have their own industry associations, research institutions, and

Talent management and career management are not the same thing

professional groups, and these are often very separate from the human resources community. As talent management has evolved inside organizations, the emphasis has been on how to leverage the workforce to best serve businesses' needs, and companies usually tell employees they are responsible for their own careers. But as in previous decades, it is usually the company that defines one's career path, as well as the boundaries and the possibilities that describe an employee's options for remaining in the organization. Few companies have provided meaningful tools for employees to take ownership of their own careers and frontline managers commonly receive little to no career theory, model, ethics, or communications training when they transition to management roles. Yet, frontline managers will have more career conversations than any other employee or, in fact, any other leader in the organization. Even the most formal talent-management programs and tools have not prepared managers with the career competency they need to wisely counsel the employees they manage. And it's been that way for a long time, even before career paths, patterns, time lines, and ownership began to shift. Today, recognizing that organizational leaders need deeper career competency is a first step to understanding the broader context of workforce and demographic change.

Observations from the Field

Talent management takes a company-first approach to the way employees support organizational goals. It is part of formal workforce planning, and while it evaluates the needs of the business, it assesses how best to optimize work by aligning the resources available inside and outside the organization. Career management (also called career development) is focused on the individual. It is the lifelong application of an individual's interests and talents. CERIC, Canada's leading career-focused institution, has defined the following eight principles of career development to help those outside the sector better understanding what good career management entails.

According to CERIC's Eight Guiding Principles of Career Development,* career development:

- is a lifelong process of blending and managing paid and unpaid activities: learning (education), work (employment, entrepreneurship), volunteerism and leisure time;
- entails determining interests, beliefs, values, skills and competencies – and connecting those with market needs;
- involves understanding options, navigating with purpose and making informed choices;
- should be self-directed: an individual is responsible for his or her own career, but is not alone – we all influence and are influenced by our environment;
- is often supported and shaped by educators, parents, peers, managers and the greater community;
- means making the most of talent and potential, however you define growth and success – not necessarily linear advancement;
- can be complex and complicated, so context is key – there may be both internal constraints (financial, cultural, health) or external constraints (labor market, technology);
- and is dynamic, evolving and requires continuous adaptation and resilience through multiple transitions. (CERIC 2016)

---

* The authors' understanding of career development is informed by various theories, many of which are summarized in the 2019 book *Career Theories and Models at Work: Ideas for Practice*, edited by Nancy Arthur, Mary McMahon, and Roberta Neault.

We believe that in the workplace as in the world, an incalculable number of forces are creating the turmoil we are currently confronting – a muddle that has spawned a number of persistent myths undermining businesses' ability to do business. Once these stresses are understood, and the myths they have generated exposed, they'll cease to be a cause for the gnashing of teeth and instead become positive factors in strategic planning.

For the first time in recent memory, longevity is requiring both organizations and individuals to rethink old models and embrace dramatic change. Author and HR strategist Peter Cappelli (2014) argues that traditional corporate approaches to talent management assume career stages and progression based on age that simply no longer reflect today's workplaces. Furthermore, Cappelli contends that these approaches are now not merely failing but extremely costly. And while we recognize myriad factors contributing to the unpredictability of today's workplaces, including new technologies, different jobs, industry consolidation, financial instability, and more, we argue that the most significant and immediate cause for instability is demographics. Every single day from now until 2031, ten thousand Americans will turn sixty-five and will either have left the organizations they have worked for or will be under pressure to do so (Cohn and Taylor 2010). At present, most organizations do not have career paths and talent programs that consider the value of an aging workforce. On the contrary, this cohort is often treated like a failing limb to be humanely amputated. What's more, since the passage of the American social security law in 1935, when average life expectancy was 61.7 years, employees have spent their working lives accepting 65 as a *finish line* (United States Congress 1985). Keep in mind, there is a difference between aging and aged. Obviously, we are all aging every day. But "aged" is a descriptor generally reserved for people nearing the end of life.

Today, sixty-five is not the same as it was understood even one generation ago. With average life expectancy reaching into the mid-eighties, organizations and individuals who assume productivity ends around sixty-five are missing out on possibly their greatest opportunity for innovation, productivity, and contribution. Research results are slow in coming. From the time it takes to design a project, secure funding, connect with subjects, gather data, analyze the data, and publish the findings, several years can pass. Practitioners' must be quicker if they are to be effective in a changing landscape, and in their book *The Aging Workforce*, published by the American Psychological Association, Hedge, Borman, and Lammlein (2006) conclude, as we do, that workers over the age of sixty, thanks to their professional expertise, will continue to make important contributions to their organizations. But it is the boomers who comprise that sector of the workforce currently thought to be aging out – a sentiment with which we do not agree. Boomers are mature workers with a great deal more to contribute than is presently understood. Indeed, it is the mature workforce that comprises the most undervalued and underused corporate resource. Equally important, we believe this underestimated group is both the primary cause and the solution for much of today's workplace disruption.

Fact 3: Changing Career Patterns Affect All Demographic Cohorts

It is often reported that millennials are true technophiles and the best cohort equipped to grapple with the technology that is changing our world. It is also widely held that millennials have transformed the workplace because of their natural affinity to technology and their tendency for prioritizing life balance over company or career loyalty (Ng, Schweitzer, and Lyons 2010). Millennials are also commonly described as entitled, optimistic, achievement-oriented, risk-averse, unfocused, and attention-craving. They are portrayed as believing they are "right" and thinking they can solve the problems preceding generations have failed to solve. What's more, they are reputed to be less loyal to an employer than their predecessors and quick to quit – usually, in search of an opportunity that better meets their needs. In short, millennials are understood to be a stimulus to change, and organizations are taking drastic steps to accommodate them. Companies embrace millennials as change-makers and are willing to do backflips on their account. Conversely, boomers are stereotypically described as focused, materialistic workaholics. It doesn't seem to matter that generalizations are typically unreliable, because perceptions have power. And even while valuing boomers as the repository of organizational knowledge, companies tend to ignore them as a talent resource.

Of course, millennials are not the first group to upset the status quo. In the past, other entrants to the workforce questioned the hierarchical structure that existed and the way that work was done. Only a few decades ago, members of Generation X were labeled the "slacker generation." Before them, boomers were identified as the "counterculture." The difference between what is happening today and previous expressions of youthful challenge is the organizational response to those expressions. There are good reasons why smart organizations are attempting to respond to the needs of young employees rather than assuming this new generation will simply fall in line over time. The sheer size of the millennial workforce – larger than the boomer population in Canada and other jurisdictions – prompts smart organizations to pay attention to them. But in their efforts to minimize turnover and create a welcoming workplace, many organizations focus primarily on this new and demanding cohort in an effort to please them.

Some generational assumptions are characteristics of youth, and at some time were part of every cohort's narrative.

However, we don't believe millennials are the most significant factor affecting today's workforces and workplaces. We contend that they are to be considered, of course, but merely as part of the overall ecosystem. Millennials are not the primary drivers of the changes we see, nor are they the answer to the difficulties those changes have produced. And that's where the problem lies.

An important corollary to organizations' overemphasis on adjusting for millennials is the associated undervaluing of mature workers within their existing employee base, plus the shortsighted and narrow focus on knowledge transfer, a subject we address more thoroughly in chapter 7. Yes, there is universal acceptance that older employees have significant knowledge to share; they are often considered the keepers of corporate memory, and may be prized for this characteristic, if not others. Less well understood is that they also have significant contributions to make well beyond merely transferring what they know to the next generation. To paraphrase Mark Twain, reports of their retreat from organizational life have been greatly exaggerated.

Zooming out brings the bigger picture – i.e., all generations – into focus.

Just as millennials are not *the* answer, neither are boomers the answer all on their own. The value lies in connecting all the generations, including the poor, forgotten Gen Xers.

Indeed, while our work, approaches, and perspectives highlight the boomer generation's significant role, we explore their role within an intergenerational construct, not a multigenerational one. As Brownell and Resnick (2005) indicate, these terms are often used interchangeably, despite the fact that they are not universally considered synonymous. Where multigenerational approaches seek to identify and isolate the generations based on their differences, intergenerational approaches looks at what becomes possible only when all cohorts are valued and considered. While there may be, in fact, generational differences, we don't want to overstate or twist them to reach faulty conclusions. It is a zero-sum game in a multigenerational organization, and resources are allocated to one group at the expense of another. In an intergenerational organization, investing in cross-generational programs allows employees of all ages to benefit.

> **Observations from the Field**
>
> Today, the dominant narrative includes the term "the multigenerational workforce." We advocate a shift in language to reflect a more accurate perspective and suggest the term "intergenerational workforce" is preferable. "Multi" highlights the many different generations, focusing on layers, numbers, and differences among them. "Inter" embraces the relationship between the generations and implies a matrix created by those relationships.

New Work-Life Stage Alters Career Time Lines

The extension of the average life span has produced myriad corollaries, and much has been written about the emergence of a new stage of life. Canadian researcher Dr. Suzanne Cook describes this new life stage as a time of "redirection" (Cook 2015).

In his book *The Big Shift*, Marc Freedman (2011) called for a recognition of what he calls "encore careers" – where the potential of the fifty-and-older workforce is harnessed to solve some of the world's greatest challenges. Since its publication, Freedman and Encore.org, the organization he founded, has collaborated on, consulted with, and curated programs that prepare those who are fifty and older to transition into social-purpose, community-based roles. The result is an increasing number of "EncoreU" programs at more than fifteen of America's most prestigious institutions, including Columbia, Cornell, Harvard, and Stanford Universities (Encore.org 2017).

Encore.org and its affiliated partners and organizations are examples of the social-change organizations referenced in chapter 1, which emerge when change is not limited to one organization, sector, or region, but instead is part of broader social change.

Until now, most of these programs and research mandates have focused on longevity's effects on individuals, and they have resulted in a plethora of playbooks, workshops, and tip sheets designed to help aging boomers reinvent themselves in their fifties, sixties, and beyond. But there a limited number of mainstream resources are aimed at helping organizations capitalize on all this reinvention. While the labor-supply side of the equation recognizes boomers as a source of new economic *capacity*, workplaces have not adjusted their

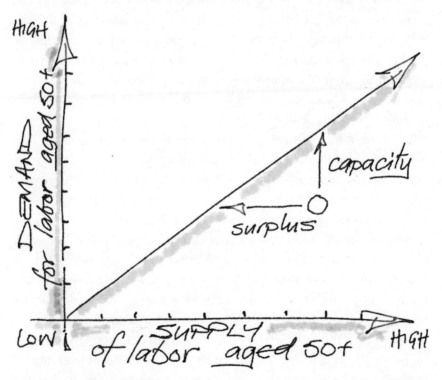

Surplus- vs. Capacity-Focused Responses to Increased Supply of Labor Aged Fifty and Older

view of later-career engagement. Instead, they remaining fixated on solving the problem of a perceived labor *surplus*.

Before we turn to the strategic shifts organizations can make to capitalize on untapped talent capacity, it's important to recognize the impact longevity has had on individual careers. It used to be that you worked until you were eligible for a pension, somewhere around sixty or sixty-five, and then you retired. In retirement, common wisdom said, you stepped back from active workforce involvement and focused on family, friends, community, and your own affairs. Whether you were a blue-collar worker or white-collar professional, you were now free to indulge in purely pleasurable activities. Perhaps you'd join a bowling league, enroll in an astronomy course, or travel the world. You might try writing, take up bridge, consider buying an RV, or decide to try your hand at sculpture. Whatever followed your working life, with only a few years left on the horizon, retirement was understood to be a last opportunity to let go and have fun. Universities ramped up their continuing education programs. Cruise lines added to their fleets. Retirement communities grew like kudzu in the South.

It is certain that this romantic notion of retirement was never uniformly true. Still, it was believed to be true, even though there were and are many examples of successful companies with founders who were in their fifties, sixties, and beyond when their companies were first launched – proving that the retirement life stage was never carved in stone. However, what is certainly true is that longevity has altered today's life course, with most people now expecting to live decades longer than the traditional age of retirement. Today, there is considerable discussion about the aging workforce; it is frequently the central theme of conferences, seminars, and boardroom meetings. But the emphasis is often misdirected. Longevity's impact on productivity is more important than its impact on the statistical average age of the workforce. It's about increased capacity, not lengthened chronological age.

Retirement has
its own
mythology.

In the 1930s, Social Security was enacted in the United States and an age was set to define one's eligibility for the benefits associated with retirement. At the time, life expectancy was just under sixty-two years, and the retirement age was set at sixty-five. Today, workers in their fifties, sixties, seventies, and beyond rarely follow the traditional models of retirement that require withdrawal from the workforce. Nor do they experience age-related decline until much later in life. As a result, a new phase of working life has emerged. We call it the Legacy Career phase (Taylor 2017a and 2017b).

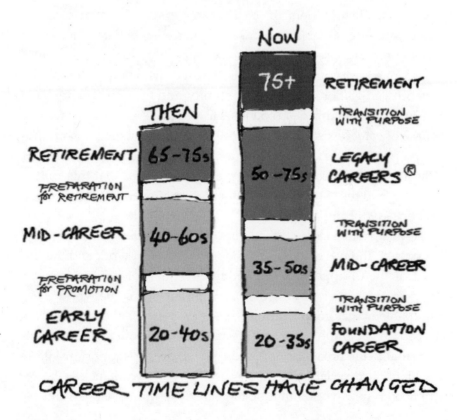

NOW

75+   RETIREMENT

TRANSITION WITH PURPOSE

50-75s   LEGACY CAREERS®

TRANSITION WITH PURPOSE

35-50s   MID-CAREER

TRANSITION WITH PURPOSE

20-35s   FOUNDATION CAREER

THEN

RETIREMENT   65-75s

PREPARATION for RETIREMENT

MID-CAREER   40-60s

PREPARATION for PROMOTION

EARLY CAREER   20-40s

CAREER TIME LINES HAVE CHANGED

Where Freedman's encore careers focus on volunteer and nonprofit-sector work, Legacy Careers have a broader definition. With decades of experience and service committed to a particular industry, job, company, and/or role, the Legacy Career phase recognizes that the mid-career phase is followed by a new career phase. Donald Super's (1957) definitive work on life-stage-based career models ends at age sixty-five. Dr. Cook's doctoral thesis (2015) and subsequent work added a new phase to Super's model, called "redirection." We see redirection as the critical activity required to enable a successful Legacy Career.

People who are able, and who are supported through a process of reimaging, redefining, and redirecting their work, can enjoy very successful and a rewarding Legacy Career. For some, there are many choices, while for others, the options are limited. Often, discussions about later-life career transitions are criticized as elitist because they apply only to those who can choose a next step from a position of financial security, as opposed to individuals who may be limited by finances, education, or local opportunity, and therefore do not have the luxury of making a job change. However, we assert that this new phase of career exists for everyone. As we live longer, we shift into a new phase of life that is different from mid-life. The success of this transition depends on two things: early awareness that this shift is coming, and the commitment, from both employers and employees, to be ready for this change.

As in any other career phase, almost everyone can "transition with purpose." Today's discussions about the future of work and the impact of the disappearance of certain jobs are not limited to older workers. However, underlying assumptions that some workers are incapable of making transitions – because they are in certain sectors or certain geographies, or with certain levels of education – are detrimental to the broader population. Given proper support, frontline cashiers, factory laborers, and other "at risk" workers can be retrained for new work. But first, there must be widespread awareness of the need for appropriate support. Employees need new tools if they are to become aware of the risks they face and the options available to them. Employers need a new understanding of how to capitalize on the shifts in the workforce by encouraging better career competency and career development skills in frontline managers.

Observations from the Field

Transitioning with purpose is a career competency that has become an essential skill. Whereas in previous generations employees prepared for their next career step within the confines of the structure their companies provided, today's employees usually have more control and more options available to them. Individuals need to be able to identify their own key career criteria based on their current needs, talents, areas of interest, and the market. While an individual's list of criteria might change over time, the exercise of identifying principles, evaluating options, and choosing the next career direction is as valuable to the new graduate as it is to the mid-career professional returning to the workforce after an extended absence, or to workers aged fifty and over who find they have fallen out of love with their work.

 Even though we are living longer, the mid-career phase has not lengthened; rather, a new career phase has emerged.

A career is bigger than a job or a role. It is comprised of a portfolio of activities. To enjoy a fulfilling Legacy Career, individuals must evaluate how they want to spend their time across a spectrum of stability-providing work arrangements and life-enhancing hobbies and interests, whether these are full time, part time, seasonal, or flexible. A career also includes entrepreneurial or risky ventures that may or may not lead to new work arrangements in the future.

Career paths and patterns are shifting as we transition from a society that prepares for our next career steps to a society that "transitions with purpose" continuously, over the length of a career – a lifetime that actually fits today's life-expectancy models.

Organizations Must Adjust to New Career Realities

Many organizations have been encouraging boomers to take a new interest in their career paths. From the AARP's "Life Reinvented" initiative to Canada's National Institute on Ageing, there is an abundance of messaging and programming for individuals. And yet, at the same time as there is little capacity-building within organizations. As a result, despite daily media hype about the importance of the boomer cohort, there is an increasing gap between boomers who are disenchanted with the limited options available to them in the workplace, and workplaces that misinterpret boomer's disenchantment and griping as signposts on the aging downslide and an indicator that they have outlived their usefulness to the organization.

In part 2, we'll debunk the most common myths about this group of aging workers – that they are more costly, less productive, and more fragile than their juniors. While most organizations buy into these myths about this cohort, and struggle with strategies for offloading them, studies and statistics prove those organizations utterly wrong. Gary Burtless of the Brookings Institution reports on a recent study by the US Social Security Administration to learn whether older workers have had a negative impact on productivity over the last twenty-five years (Burtless 2013). According to Burtless, the study found that this is not the case, and he suggests that companies would do well to increase rather than decrease their reliance on their aging workers. Burtless is not alone. Pierre Cléroux, chief economist at the Business Development Bank of Canada, foresees a labor shortage as boomers retire and fewer young people are available to fill their shoes (Business Development Bank of Canada 2013). He emphasizes the experience and generally strong work ethic of older workers, and suggests that this population is best suited to solve the problem of a forthcoming labor crunch. Cléroux argues that if businesses think employees have nothing to contribute after sixty-five, they are way out of date and had better do some serious rethinking.

The reasons for researchers and business experts' conviction that older workers offer an advantage rather than a weakness are as many and varied as the skills and talents within the aging workforce (Van Dalen, Henkens, and Schippers 2010). In fact, by every current business benchmark, research demonstrates that the productivity, drive, and contribution of older employees who choose to stay in the workforce compares positively with their younger coworkers. And where there may be some element of cognitive decline, new technology and a wealth of experience makes up for it.

These are the boomers – the mature population – healthier, more driven, and more energetic at sixty-five and older than ever before in history. They are often more people-savvy than their juniors and comprise a rich mine of talent – one that is already on the payroll. In 2011, what Statistics Canada terms "mature workers" (aged fifty-five and older) accounted for upwards of 18 percent of the Canadian workforce (Statistics Canada 2014).

Since human capital costs generally amount to 70 percent of operational expenses, failing to adequately use this segment of the available talent pool is extremely expensive.

But most organizations are only just beginning to assess what to do with their mature workers (Cook and Rougette 2017). For those that have tackled the issue, career paths, talent programs, and workforce planning are generally based on outdated assumptions – assumptions more in keeping with 1935, when sixty-five was deemed the designated retirement age.

Observations from the Field

A while back Taylor was sitting with a group of people from Canada and the United Kingdom, all aged fifty and older. Unprompted, they began discussing the UK government's move to shift the age of state pension eligibility to seventy. Surprised, one woman blurted out, "Can you imagine?" Then she demonstrated what it would sound like when a client called the company. She imitated a seventy-year-old receptionist with a shaky voice and total confusion with a caller's request.

The group laughed until Taylor pointed out that in this very group there were many people over seventy, none of whom sounded feeble or were easily confused. It was an important observation because ageism is so deeply rooted in our culture that even when we ourselves are within the age range of the cohort being discussed, we allow stereotypes to inform our view of reality. Even when the stereotype contradicts what we know to be true from our own experience, we tend to accept it.

Equally important and most often overlooked, research demonstrates a direct correlation between education and the wish to retire: the more educated the employee, the later the retirement age (Paullin 2014). In terms of an employee's value to the organization, research shows that mature employees who defer retirement are likely to be better educated, more skilled, and more motivated than the general workforce population. According to a recent report from the SHRM, "mature workers – generally defined as workers over age 50 or 55 – have experience and skills honed during decades of employment. Retaining talented mature workers – and recruiting new ones – is simply good business for most organizations" (Paullin 2014).

So instead of packaging them out or developing programs to ease them into retirement, it's time to design new strategies to embrace the veteran population, engage their interests, use their talents, and leverage their strengths. It's time to recognize the opportunity for building a lasting workforce advantage – and to profit from it.

Ageism: The Last Socially Acceptable Form of Discrimination

Observations from the Field

One of Lebo's clients was Jack, director of sales, Canada, for a Fortune 500 global communications company. He left the company's employ at sixty-six, tired of explaining to US management why Canadians were different from Americans and why US sales methods were not ideal for the Canadian market. And despite scoring well according to company metrics, he felt he'd never really succeeded in getting the company to deliver what Canadian buyers wanted. Jack knew the company's primary goal was IPOs, and that long-term sales and service were less important than quick revenue, and he believed he hadn't served his customers as well as he might – an ongoing source of frustration.

Jack is a caring people-person, and he'd come to feel his integrity was at stake. As a trained engineer, inveterate problem-solver, and habitual innovator, Jack had a number of suggestions to offer. He spoke with management to see if he might work in a different capacity – one he believed would be of serious benefit to the company. Since he knew Canadian buyers, he offered to take a pay cut and suggested a "part time" position where he'd work on implementation, planning, and follow-up services. The company wasn't interested. He suggested a number of innovative projects targeting Canadian buyers. They refused. He recommended several other possibilities that would leverage his insights, skills, and expertise. They turned him down.

The positions Jack was inventing did not exist, and he didn't know whether the company feared setting a precedent or saw no value in his suggestions. But either way, they appeared to be inflexible. Feeling he'd had enough, Jack handed in his resignation, to the dismay of management, who were happy to keep him on board in his original position.

After sixteen months of retirement Jack realized that his prime motivator had always been problem-solving for the people he served. Whether in direct sales or a leadership role, his kicks came from helping people find ways to get where they wanted to go. So, like many others in his shoes, Jack took a job at Home Depot. Now he's using his passion for woodworking and his talent for innovation to help people get where they're going. The lower pay is not an issue, and, happily, the job keeps him smiling. The company Jack used to work for has lost an opportunity.

Whether companies intend to be ageist or not is irrelevant. Ageist language, beliefs, and norms are so much a part of today's culture that they are often overlooked, dismissed, or defended. As aging activist Ashton Applewhite indicates in her book *This Chair Rocks* (2016), ageism is a part of our everyday experience, from greeting someone by saying they look "good for their age," to the hundreds of comments and jokes that reinforce someone's age as a source for declining ability.

Observations from the Field

In the fall of 2016, Taylor attended an evening symposium focused on combating sexism in politics and finding ways to increase the number of women in Canadian political leadership by the year 2020.

Among the panelists was then minister for the status of women, the Honorable Patty Hajdu, who remarked in closing that it was past time for younger female representation in the House of Commons. She went on to ask the audience if they had noticed how old one particular minister was. A quick Google search indicated the "old" politician was sixty-six, and as Taylor contemplated approaching the microphone to address this blatant ageism as part of a call to overcome sexism, members of the audience shouted "ageism." It was an uninvited and spontaneous audience reaction that Taylor thinks would not have been forthcoming even ten years ago. In any case, upon reading the reaction in the room, the minister defended her comment, saying she had a good relationship with the minister in question and his age was an ongoing joke between them.

In a follow-up letter to the minister, Taylor wrote: "Ageism is rampant and we don't always recognize it, even when we are a contributing party. I ask you to consider what caused you, once your comments were identified as ageist, to excuse it because it is an ongoing joke between you and Minister McCallum. Your relationship would certainly not excuse him making a sexist comment about you while on a panel."

Even those who should lead the battle against unintended ageist language often find themselves trapped in old patterns.

Organizations know they must not discriminate based on age. And yet, every day they find ways to use language to signal that applicants over forty need not apply. *Fast Company* and *Fortune* identified the growing number of companies that are now including the term "digital native" in their job postings as a way to signal their desire to find younger talent (Loehr 2016). A recent posting on Facebook for a new administrative assistant called for someone "young and hungry," not only indicating age-based hiring practices, but also falling into the trap of many of the myths we will explore in part 2 – namely that older workers are expensive, less productive, and hard to train. And while current research indicates that it is not reasonable to expect homogeneity within any age cohort, we routinely treat generational groups as if they aren't made up of disparate individuals (Lyons and Schweitzer 2016). Organizations apply stereotypes to age cohorts and make decisions based on labels, so it is important to expose age-associated myths.

Observations from the Field

Todd was a client of Lebo's who began to detect signs of ageism at work shortly after his fiftieth birthday. With an engineering degree and a PhD in human factors, Todd was much more than an ordinary website architect; he was a user-experience choreographer.

Todd was smart, creative, and seriously talented. He'd won several design awards and had been turning down headhunters for years. A health issue prevented him from accepting the offer of a senior VP position where he worked, but he was happy as a middle manager in a high-tech consulting agency and he enjoyed his role as leader, creative thinker, and coach. His clients loved him and his designs routinely won international awards.

While the younger members on his team were technically skilled, Todd began to notice that many of them wanted to make changes only for the sake of change – a strategy with which he did not agree. He pointed out that many of the changes they'd previously suggested resulted in no improvement in usability or aesthetics. He reminded his team that several of the changes to which he'd acquiesced had frustrated end users – and they'd complained loudly. Todd insisted that good design required every change to improve the user's experience, not to confuse them.

But Todd's boss, a new VP ten years Todd's junior, did not agree. He liked the idea of continuous change for its own sake, and he

---

thought the users should get used to it. He also thought Todd should "get with it" because it was billable work and it was "cool."

Todd didn't think it was cool, and he soon realized he was being overlooked for new projects. "The younger guys can handle it," his boss said. "They'll be fine without you." Another time, the boss's comment was even more pointed: "We need some fresh ideas," he said. Todd began to feel marginalized and he suspected he was being set up to be let go with a "suddenly stupid" label on his file.

Todd began to look for another job, only to find that the more than two decades of experience on his CV instantly eliminated him from every job post that should have had his name on it. In fact, he didn't get a single callback.

At a party one night, Todd met a headhunter who told him he'd never send a candidate over forty-five to a high-tech client. "Too old," he said. "My clients wouldn't be happy. You have to be young to really get the tech stuff, y'know?" That's what the headhunter said, because that's what he believed.

Todd removed the damning detail from his résumé and received an interview with his first submission. Of course, he got the job – just ahead of a pink slip.

Age and Technology

It is impossible to write about the future of work and changing workplace dynamics without acknowledging the impact of rapid technological advancement. There are daily discussions about which jobs will remain in an increasingly automated future. The Technology Revolution has started to deliver on its initial promise to automate, connect, and transform the way work is done. With email, Skype, clouds, virtual collaboration spaces, apps, and wearable technology, we can be productive anywhere, any time. With robots instead of human hands fulfilling orders, answering calls, or placing the spare tire in a car rolling off the assembly line, we see yet more examples of automation replacing people. That said, this book is not about technology. It's about the impact of the demographic shift on the workplace. Our interest is where age-based assumptions or demographic stereotypes regarding technology limit the potential of organizations to capitalize on opportunity. That is the future of work.

We hear comments about boomers' limited technological abilities all the time, and while it is true that younger generations have been born into a tech-enabled world, most boomers have migrated to today's technology with only a slight accent to indicate it's not their mother tongue. In fact, most make a serious effort to stay ahead of the curve, realizing that if they do not, they will be marked as archaic.

Observations from the Field

Walking through a shopping mall recently, Lebo stopped at a phone kiosk to ask for directions. A pleasant young man at the counter helpfully pointed the way before asking if he could tempt her with a new phone.

"No thanks," she said. "I'm happy with the one I've got."

"Is it a flip phone?" he asked.

Lebo started to walk away, but eager to hear the explanation for the young man's guess, she turned back and asked what would make him think she had a flip phone.

"Well," he explained, "at a certain age most people are intimidated by technology and the new phones confuse them, so they use flip phones." Lebo looked skeptical.

"That's what the service providers would tell you if you asked," he continued. "Check it out. Most older people use flip phones. It's a fact."

Maybe his theory kicks in at the century mark, but Lebo couldn't think of a single friend, colleague, or peer who uses a flip phone – not one! And they are mostly of "a certain age." The young man's comment had annoyed her and the exchange highlighted the problem with stereotypes: they're so often dead wrong.

"That's the dumbest thing I've ever heard," she said.

This shift in where work gets done is as true for the sixty-two-year-old sales representative who logs sales calls on an app on his smart phone and logs in from home on nights and weekends as it is for the twenty-five-year-old marketing associate who has actually been to the office a mere handful of times in the past six months.

Obviously, technology has changed the way we work and who does the work. There is also an associated assumption that technology is a de facto replacement for people and that because of technology an incalculable number of jobs have been lost. And while it is true that technology does in fact replace people, it is also true that it has simultaneously created an incalculable number of jobs for people who must support the new technologies. As jobs change and shift there is, more than ever, a need for all employees to see a path forward and learn how to transition with purpose.

> Even non-native users of technology can become tech proficient.

Observations from the Field

Recently, Taylor spent an afternoon with the general manager of a manufacturing plant. In their discussion, the GM told Taylor that technology was creating a significant skill shortage that would be one of his top talent priorities for the next few years. Equipment at the plant had not been updated in a long time and was therefore no longer considered "current." Moreover, there would be no significant upgrades to the old technology for a few years, and in the meantime, there were hundreds of unfilled positions because it was impossible to attract and retain new graduates in a technologically archaic environment. It was a tough situation compounded by hiring competition from a new power plant within two hundred kilometers that needed similar skills.

Technology was driving a case for a mid- and late-career hiring strategy with a recognition that millennials might never work in core roles. The long-term career considerations were significant. Historically, a worker rose through the ranks from a hands-on role in the business, and if millennials refused roles that provided a frontline understanding of the functioning of the plant, how could they be effective in the future as leaders of the company? Or, could there be some short-term solution using boomers to maintain the plants while a long-term plan targeted Generation Z – a cohort just starting to graduate from high school?

Today's workplace is not focused on where work gets done or how it is financed. Neither is it focused on how operations are optimized. Instead, it focuses on who does what work in part because of what HR researcher Josh Bersin calls a "global talent deficit" (Bersin 2012). According to Bersin and other researchers, millennials' preparation, experience and skill sets are in the main insufficient for them to excel in today's demanding workplace. While they may possess raw talent and have highly polished skills in a number

 The Technology Revolution has enabled a more human revolution.

of areas, the deficit, it seems, is in the so-called soft skills – skills generally honed with experience. If organizations want to capitalize on the shifting workforce, the singular focus on talent needs to give way to enhanced career competency and more sophisticated thinking.

Not Your Parents' Workplace

Today's workplace is not the same as the one your parents entered. Nor, if you are over forty, is it the same workplace as the one you entered. We are living through times of significant change, and these changes are more deeply personal than in past revolutionary waves. The talent revolution challenges the nature of our own work, our own value, and the collective impact workforces have in organizations across our economy.

Being part of this revolution is not optional. In the next few chapters we'll demonstrate the significant changes that affect every workplace. Whether your organization chooses to be revolutionary in its approach to talent, or whether it becomes a casualty of the revolution, is up to you. There are risks associated with being an early adopter of new trends and there are even greater risks in being a laggard, waiting too long to recognize the time for change.

 The talent revolution is not optional, and your participation in it is time-sensitive.

This is your Goldilocks moment. It is not too early to join the revolution. Nor is it too late. The timing is just right. Indeed, for those wishing to capitalize on an aging workforce the time for change is now. Yes, it is sometimes painful. But we contend that as talent emerges as the great business disruptor of the next decade, unlimited opportunities will emerge for individuals and for the organizations that employ them.

This is a never-before-seen work space where thought leaders will build new models that leverage the strengths found within a new reality – and there are plenty of strengths going to waste, even as we watch. These strengths are not invisible; they must simply be revealed. For companies seeking a competitive advantage, we propose a new and different understanding of demographics and workplace transformation, and a different approach to the changes underway. We propose recognizing this tumultuous era and naming it for what it really is: a talent revolution.

Key Points

- Old workforce expectations are no longer reliable; the arc of careers has changed.
- Ageism is insidious, rampant, and stifling in today's world of work.
- We must adjust to new career realities to take advantage of untapped opportunities for growth and profit.
- Your participation in the talent revolution is time-sensitive.

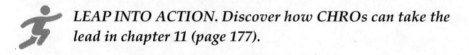 *LEAP INTO ACTION. Discover how CHROs can take the lead in chapter 11 (page 177).*

4

AN ORGANIZATIONAL LENS: THE BROKEN TALENT ESCALATOR

To add another dimension to the analysis of your environment and improve workforce planning, it is important to understand your current career model vis-à-vis workforce demographics. This chapter explores the opportunities, barriers, and influences created by the traditional corporate career model.

Right now, the corporate ladder isn't working. In fact, it is immovable, formalized, and clogged, which makes it obsolete. And whether it's a building or a corporate career model, an obsolete structure must be either renovated or demolished. Based on the inflexibility of the current corporate career model and its poor fit with changing workforce demographics, and comparing the outdated career-path paradigm with the success of our proposed strategies, we're convinced the current model is a teardown.

To demonstrate the impact the career revolution is already having on your organization, we present the image of a Broken Talent Escalator before showing you why it broke down and what a Broken Talent Escalator is costing you.

Your Broken Talent Escalator

Today's organizational career models are built on a number of institutional practices that are wildly out of step with the changing workforce. The principal assumption is that if you're good at your job and work hard, you'll rise within the organization because the organization is paternalistic and can be counted on to look after your interests. But the pendulum has swung. Career ownership once again rests in the hands of the worker, and traditional workplace career-path structures no longer function as expected (Lyons et al. 2012). If they did, job-hopping would not have become the new normal for millennials (Meister 2012). Indeed, according to Amy Adkins (2016), a writer at Gallup, those itchy feet translate to six in ten millennials being open to quitting their job for an opportunity elsewhere. It seems likely that if workers could rely on steadily moving up throughout their working life, millennials would tend to stay with the same employer until retirement, or at least they would stay considerably longer than they currently do. But the fact is, most move on after only a few dozen months (US Bureau of Labor Statistics 2018).

Statistics Canada breaks down job tenure in a dozen different categories and the US Bureau of Labor Statistics (2018) reports that these days the median length of time workers stay with the same employers is 4.3 years for men and 4.0 years for women. In a recent online *Forbes* article, Jeanne Meister (2013) reported on a survey of 1,189 employees and 150 managers by MultipleGenerations@Work that revealed that 91 percent of millennials expect to stay in a job for less than three years – which adds up to a staggering 15 to 20 jobs over the course of their working life. It's worth noting that when they were young, boomers changed jobs with about the same frequency, but the switch from one job to another was usually made within the same organization, so the optics were different; it looked like they had more staying power. To be fair, today's job-hopping may be more about millennials' youth than proof of a cohort characteristic (Lyons and Kuron 2013). Nevertheless, the speed with which millennials quit is a realistic concern for the companies for which they work.

> Frequent job change has always been common in early-stage careers.

What's more, if current workplace career paths played out effectively for employers, North American companies would not consider offloading mature workers an urgent need. They would stop thinking of their mature workers as high-cost, low-reward employees who are clogging the system and keeping potentially productive workers waiting on the sidelines. All employees would be equally valued as contributing members until the day of their retirement. But companies *do* want to offload their older workers – and the faster, the better. And even though age discrimination is illegal, it is so deeply rooted that documenting extensive experience on one's résumé can be a dog whistle alerting recruiters and HR managers against hiring (Applewhite 2016). The harsh reality is that, because organizations fail to use their entire workforce effectively, too often talent either stagnates or leaves.

We use the metaphor of an escalator to describe the current workplace career model because everyone can visualize an escalator as a moving staircase with treads that carry people at a constant speed upwards. Individuals can choose to step faster than the system moves, but only if there is space on the step above. We ask you to consider today's workplace career structure as a talent escalator: we assert that this escalator is broken. Furthermore, we blame the greater part of today's workplace dissatisfaction on a Broken Talent Escalator. Indeed, we submit that your organization has a Broken Talent Escalator too.

The talent escalator we present is not to be confused with the corporate ladder. On our escalator, a person's upward career progression is based on time, not on professional advancement. Regardless of position or rank, everyone rides the escalator for as long as they are engaged as an employee. And in the world of talent plans, fixed career paths, and pension structures, the escalator is simply too short. It does not match the reality that longevity adds to the equation. It ends long before employees are finished contributing to the workplace.

Even if your strategic thinking is exceptional and you've achieved the transformational implementation of new and groundbreaking programs, we know there are hidden talent pools and structural anachronisms that prevent you from capitalizing on the full potential of your workforce. We know it because we see it every day.

Picture this. When an employee is hired, she steps onto the first tread of the escalator and, as her career progresses, she steps up to the next tread. Occasionally, someone behind may move up and past her towards the top, but overall, the system keeps moving and everyone progresses upward at a fairly predictable rate. Should she leave, she is off the escalator with no easy way to get back on and no simple mechanism to rejoin "the team" if she wishes to do so. And so it is with an individual's career path. Until retirement approaches.

As an employee nears retirement, he is challenged less, offered less, and expected to stop trying to move up. The steps flatten out and there is an expectation that ensures that the boomer population either exits the workforce completely or stalls at the top, stepping back every time the tread disappears beneath them. It's a structure that impedes the forward progress of the workers behind and stifles talent throughout the entire system. The effect is that, whether by choice or financial circumstance, workers in their fifties and sixties return to work every day to ride the top step of the escalator like a treadmill – trapped in the same place in the same role – impeding the forward progress of younger workers, interfering with their own self-actualization, clogging the system, and affecting the entire organization.

 Your older workers are stuck on a talent treadmill.

A Broken Talent Escalator is a major business disruptor, one that knocks the entire system out of whack. It contributes to a culture of complacency and inertia, and can create pockets of dysfunction and distraction. It affects productivity, employee engagement, and revenue. Sadly, the very structure specifically built to enable career advancement fails to deliver as too many on board mark time.

Observations from the Field

The word "career" originates from the Latin word *carrus*, which refers to a wagon, cart, or chariot. The etymology makes sense, because in a cart you can travel in any direction, taking the tools and implements you need. In today's emergent state of the talent revolution it is not yet clear what analogy best replaces modern images of career ladders, lattices, jungle gyms, and now escalators. But the idea that a career is a vehicle carrying an individual in any direction they choose for any distance they choose is an appealing one (CERIC 2016).

The Reason Your Talent Escalator Is Broken

One root cause of a Broken Talent Escalator is its length. The structure is simply too short and fails to account for increased lifespans and the commensurate lengthening of individual career paths. And while many improvements in workforce design have recently emerged, there is a heavy focus on the changing nature of today's workplace, the role of automation, and what is now technologically possible – with insufficient analysis of the hidden capacity resulting from extended life spans. It is ironic that in an age when we commonly hear that time is the most valuable commodity on earth, we ignore the decades of additional time during which individuals can be productive and drive enhanced competitiveness for our organizations. What's more, additional time on the job builds a wealth of intellectual capital. Leveraging the considerable talents of your mature cohort is not an act of kindness to an aging workforce; it is the smart business thing to do. It's smart because it taps into a hidden talent pool.

 Your talent escalator is too short.

Shifting Talent off the Top Step

A second cause of a Broken Talent Escalator is known as the "lump of labor." There was a long-held belief that the number of positions in the economy is finite. If true, it means that part of the difficulty new graduates face in finding work is that older workers are not retiring "on time." Believers in the lump-of-labor concept contend that since the amount of work is limited, the only way for new entrants to enter the workforce or for others to move up into more senior roles is for someone currently holding a job to leave it. This belief has long been used to block women from entering the workforce (what will happen to the men?) or to block immigrants from coming into a given territory (how will locals find work?) (Bishop 2016).

But in 1891, the economist D.F. Schloss coined the phrase "Lump of Labor Fallacy," explaining that it's a mistake to believe that the amount of work to be done is finite. In fact, he said, the amount of work in the economy is infinite and the lump-of-labor concept is a fallacy. The "Lump of Labor Fallacy" quickly became a staple phrase in economists' lexicon. Today, economists and politicians make the argument that lump-of-labor thinking is simply wrong – that it provokes layoffs, high unemployment, anger about immigration, and bad policy decisions in both government and business. From time to time, when the economy is sluggish, the conviction that work is limited tends to resurface. Economists generally respond with derision, explaining yet again that the amount of work to be done is infinite (Bishop 2016).

When the economy took a tumble in 2008, demolishing many retirement nest-eggs and forcing countless older employees to stay in the workforce, the phrase reemerged. Boomers were blamed for clogging a sluggish system that had no room to accommodate them. But studies show that in Organisation for Economic Co-operation and Development (OECD) member countries that have increased labor force participation among older workers, youth employment also increases (Delsen and Reday-Mulvey 1996).

The weekly news magazine the *Economist* tackled the assumption that older workers' labor market participation is connected to labor market opportunities for younger workers. In their study of OECD countries, they found that there is, in fact, a correlation – but not the one they had expected to find. Indeed, the study reached a startling

 Youth employment rises when older workers are engaged appropriately.

and perhaps game-changing conclusion. It found that when older workers remained engaged in the economy longer, youth unemployment rates dropped. Apparently, more experienced labor generates jobs for less-experienced labor (The Economist 2012).

The Lump of Labor Revisited

It is now generally accepted as a mistake – a gargantuan blunder – to think that older workers will clog the whole system if they don't retire. But here's the rub: among economists today, the concept of the fallacy itself is controversial. A growing number of economists suggest that calling the lump of labor a fallacy is wrong. That is, a lump of labor that chokes the system may be very real.

We agree. Yes, in a theoretical sense there may indeed be an infinite amount of work to be done in the world, but within each company there are limited budgets for salaries and benefits, and limited positions to be filled. In the real world, as many economists are now admitting, the lump of labor may not be a fallacy at all.

But it is true that older workers can threaten the career opportunities and advancement of younger workers if they – the older workers – are not working in roles that leverage the value of their experience. For example, when an older worker takes a frontline role simply to do a job instead of using his or her depth of experience in assisting with training, development, operational efficiency, or innovative-practice development, that worker may indeed be taking a job that a new graduate could have done equally well – and at a lower cost to the organization.

The vast majority of organizations have lumps of labor currently on the top step of the escalator, and that talent needs to go somewhere. Ironically, the very people who comprise the lump are the strongest advocates for lengthening career paths, formalizing new arrangements, and developing new models.

 Allowing boomers to become a lump of labor creates a Broken Talent Escalator.

Our own informal survey confirms our hypotheses that working boomers crave opportunities to transition with purpose from the roles they are now in to different, meaningful, and appropriate roles that meet their changed needs, use their talents, ignite their passion, and are market viable – but they haven't been asked what else they could or would do. On the contrary, organizational signals indicate that they are expected to leave. It is curious that the first significant act of career ownership we see is the decision boomers en masse are making to stay put instead of acquiescing to company pressure to retire.

The Costs of a Broken Talent Escalator

The most obvious problem created by a Broken Talent Escalator is its enormous price tag. There are costs and risks associated with mismanaging any part of the talent escalator, some of which are easy to measure and appear on financial statements, others that are significant but harder to quantify, such as the effect on the brand and on employee engagement, missed opportunities, inefficiency, and productivity.

In our involvement with workforces across North America, we've learned that the majority of people who remain on this career treadmill do so because it is familiar, and while it doesn't feel good to be the employee who is stuck on the top step, it is preferable to stepping into the unknown. Still, while some remain out of fear and others out of financial need or circumstance, permitting an entire group to march in place as they age is counterproductive and undermines the very real contribution these individuals know they could be making.

As ever greater numbers of employees reach the traditional age of retirement, there is a growing crowd on the top step of the escalator. They are stuck on their step with no catalyst to move them forward. Moreover, when they march in place they reinforce the perception of limited choices and options for the people on the steps below. Eventually the backlog reaches all the way down to the first tread, where the youngest recruits are just stepping on and evaluating their interest in taking this particular route to the top.

The escalator career-path structure is antithetical to the self-actualizing millennial who is willing and eager to take responsibility for Me Inc. A new graduate looks up the length of the escalator and sees people stuck on their steps. She sees that the system ahead is congested and to assist her as she adjusts to her new role as an employee her organization may have assigned her a mentor – from the very steps that are the most crowded. But her mentor conveys subtle and not-so-subtle cues that this tedium is the norm around here, that after playing nicely in the sandbox, you don't go anywhere, and that this is an organization in which people are not fully in control of their own careers.

> **Employees stuck on the top step affect the culture of the entire workforce.**

The dissonance between a new recruit's conviction that his career is his own and the paternalistic structure of formal career paths and patterns inside the organization influence the new hire to set out cautiously. He may begin his assent and, in many cases, before riding more than one or two treads he'll abandon this path, leave the escalator, and pursue a different direction – confirmation of the common belief that millennials are quick to quit. The costs are huge (Cook and Rougette 2017). Cook and Rougette document many benefits that employers can reap by undertaking good talent-management practices with older workers, including access to better problem-solving, decision-making, lower turnover and absenteeism, and increased ability to integrate new training and learning into business practice. We will return to some of these benefits in part 2 when we dispel common workplace myths (Cook and Rougette 2017).

In 2007, the SHRM released its findings from a massive survey asking HR practitioners to look ahead and identify key priorities for the profession through 2015. The report notes that over the next several years, HR professionals expected that their number

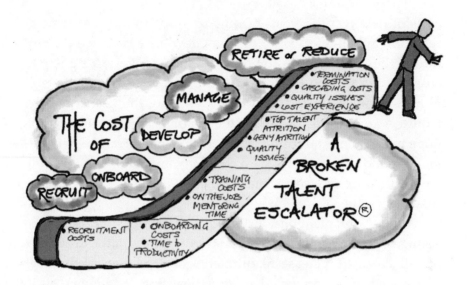

one challenge would be developing the next generation of organizational leaders (Society for Human Resource Management 2007). While that report was completed over a decade ago, it is clear that HR managers' focus would be – and is – on the youngest workers within their organizations. That said, the SHRM is amassing a series of tools and reports focused on the value of older workers with the intention of identifying best practices for retaining them. Can you afford to have your competitors get ahead of you in how to capitalize on this hidden talent pool?

In our work with more than fifty organizations across North America, we've identified the link between the costs and the risks associated with each step of the talent escalator. First, we find that the indirect or soft costs of mismanaging those employees nearing the top steps – the older workers – directly contributes to the hard costs of recruitment. In other words, the people leaving or about to leave your organization are talking about you – so they'd better be saying good things, because what they say is part of your organization's brand. Then, too, onboarding costs of new recruits, costs of time to productivity, and costs of retention are all affected by the way new hires perceive the culture. If they're being mentored by disengaged lifers, it's going to cost you big time in the long run. Next, if employers want employees to stick around, they'd best be sure the keepers of the culture – i.e., the lifers – are good examples of what new recruits hope to become. And finally, relationships matter, and when millennials and Generation Z see a company mistreating or ignoring any of their employees, it makes them wonder if this is a place they want to be.

In many organizations, priority is given to supporting the youngest employees on the lowest steps of the escalator. Resources are allocated to increase recruitment efforts, enhance employer brand, and implement innovative onboarding programs – all in an attempt to increase recent-graduate retention rates beyond their first eighteen to twenty-four months. On the surface, it makes sense that Generation Z and millennials have become a priority area of focus in talent-management strategies. Keep in mind that most organizations are bracing for a mass exodus of older workers and they are mightily concerned. They are eager to onboard new staff, and to educate, integrate, and mentor them before they lose their most seasoned employees. They also need new candidates for second-level and executive-leadership positions, and so they are placing a priority on rapid leadership development.

The entire escalator is being primed for significant changes from both the top and the bottom. It all sounds reasonable until you realize there is actually very little attention being paid to the top step and very little understanding of what is happening there. If organizations want to ensure that their workforce over the next decade is stable, sustainable, and becomes their most significant competitive advantage, they've got it backwards. They're focused on the wrong end of the escalator!

Key Points

- You have a Broken Talent Escalator.
- Your older workers are stuck on a talent treadmill.
- A Broken Talent Escalator has an enormous price tag.
- Employees stuck on the top step affect the culture of the entire workforce.
- Organizations need a new career-pathing model that is in synch with the demographics and demands of today's workforce.

 LEAP INTO ACTION. Jump to critical actions for CEOs in chapter 10 (page 164).

Part Two

EXPLODING MYTHS AND CHALLENGING UNTRUTHS

5

FROM THEORY TO PRACTICE: THE COSTS OF MYTHS AND UNTRUTHS

There is a gap between employees' desire to join the talent revolution and organizations' will to make the changes a revolution demands. That gap is filled with myths. And whether we call them myths, untruths, or downright lies, these are the impediments interfering with an organization's ability to gain a competitive advantage from their aging workforce.

In this chapter we present an approach for working through the myths and developing an intervention based on research and practice. Social psychologists study human behavior, and in the last quarter-century many have concentrated on how people form impressions of each other and make decisions based on these impressions. Researchers have studied beliefs and influences, explored attitudes and conflicts, and examined "inferential rules that people use to make judgements" (Kunda 1999, 3). It turns out that we humans suffer from a tendency to categorize others and to use these categories as pillars on which to base our beliefs and our decisions. Put another way, we use categories or stereotypes as justification for our prejudices and make decisions based on these prejudices. The three categories on which we tend to base our opinions are race, sex, and age (Kunda 1999)

Our focus here is solely on age, but it is important to realize that our tendency to stereotype people based on age breeds deeply held beliefs or myths about aging. And the stereotypes about aging workers are of serious consequence in the workplace. We might ask why these stereotypes persist, but the answers are unclear. Sometimes they are accepted as truths simply because they've been around for so long. Sometimes they are believed because, at some level, they seem to make sense. Perhaps they result from fear of the impending changes we all face without deep analysis or good data to set the record straight. In their research on making truth stick, psychologists Swartz, Newman, and Leach (2016) found that attempts to correct misinformation may actually reinforce the myth in question. Not all researchers agree. Professor J. Berger advances alternative reasons for the sharing of information (correct or otherwise), asserting that the reasons are self-serving rather than altruistic (Berger 2014). But whatever the reason, protests against change are most often proffered as "logical" objections. Unfortunately, they are *not* based on logic or on any kind of rational thinking. They are founded on biases that not only stymie creativity but result in significant and sustained resistance to organizations' attempts to ready themselves for the talent revolution.

Among the many myths that seem to float freely within our business cultures, some will dissipate over time, some will flare briefly and disappear quickly, and some will seem to be ever-present or reappear regularly like a game of whack-a-mole. The apparently permanent myths we address here have a deep and long-lasting impact on the culture in which they are found.

In our work, we have identified five "ever-present" myths. They drive counterproductive workforce strategies and shape attitudes and approaches to the aging workforce. What's more, they give people opposed to change good reason to dig their heels in, even while there is a recognition that the typical career cycle is not behaving as it used to. In most cases, as with our findings about ageism in general, executives do not set out to ignore, marginalize, or cast off segments of their employee population. But they do misinterpret some of the macro trends we have discussed thus far.

We have found that most organizations believe the following statements to be true, and even though it might not be politically correct – or even legal – to articulate them explicitly, organizations send these messages nonetheless, and they are received loud and clear by employees.

Employers believe:

- Older workers cost more than younger workers.
- It is smart business to set a "best before date" for working life.
- Training workers over a certain age is a waste of precious investment dollars.
- Older workers are less productive than younger workers.
- Performance issues are common to older workers and cannot be easily managed or remediated.

We have observed that these five myths are universally present to greater or lesser degrees in organizations in Canada and the United States. And yet, all five of these statements are untrue. What's more, each one is potentially costing organizations millions. Observation proves it. Experience proves it. Research proves it. And still these myths survive.

That the myths are pervasive is not surprising. We live in an era of fake news and alternative facts. Canadian journalist Steve Paikin recently commented that nothing is more alarming than hearing political, corporate, and community leaders say, "I don't know the facts, but here is what I think ..." (Paikin 2017). Indeed, these days what we believe to be true is often deemed as valid as what the facts prove to be true, and when it comes to older workers, we certainly see this at play. Employers believe the myths listed above are affecting their businesses without having conducted studies of their older workers. Data is in short supply but opinions are strong, a dangerous foundation for strategy.

Sometimes the presence or impact of these falsehoods is hard to identify or quantify. In our work, we take an "objection-needs"-based approach to dig deeper than symptoms, so we can construct strategies and tactics that address the root causes. In the following chapters we discuss these myths in detail.

In each case, we've spent hours listening to organizational leaders express concerns and objections – their rationales for why Broken Talent Escalators cannot be fixed, why it is imprudent to train older workers, why older workers are so costly. We've analyzed the myths and come to the clear realization that each is propelled by an underlying corporate need. These underlying needs must be acknowledged and addressed as part of any workable solution, or the organization is unlikely to see a benefit from any new initiative.

Some Serious Myth-Busting!

Observations from the Field

Business and career coach Michael Ehling has long championed the classic technique of flipping objections into needs. Objections are often emotional or nonlogical reasons for why a particular change cannot or should not occur. Ehling calls these objections "Yeah, buts," a phrase commonly used to block change. The "Yeah, but" is often articulated by someone saying, "Yeah, but ... if we did x, then y would happen, so it won't work." You may even have noticed a few "Yeah, buts" of your own as you read through these pages.

Google "Yeah, but" and you'll come up with more than a million results, which speaks to the power of the phrase. "Yeah, buts," or objections in general, are incredibly valuable because they point us to areas where more data is needed and where new approaches to problem-solving should be applied. Merely refuting the "Yeah, but" can leave the objector feeling put down or dismissed, whereas flipping the phrase stimulates constructive thinking. Typically, within each objection there are several – sometimes many – hidden, unarticulated needs. By confronting the objection and reframing the statement to begin with "We need," new opportunities for problem-solving emerge.

A long list of needs sets the parameters of a project or the criteria for making decisions. Where there was only resistance, there is now commitment to finding new solutions and meeting everyone's needs.

Objections can be reframed into specific, articulated needs.

With these needs identified, we turn to the common themes that help organizations handle the objections so that multiple myths can be addressed and demolished at the same time. You'll see that all the needs across all the myths fit within at least one of four key action areas.

The four key action areas comprise the following requirements:

1 Update organizational thinking and mindset about careers and longevity.

2 Individualize talent-management and career-path programs; avoid "generation-based" assumptions as a foundation for employee grouping.
3 Ensure you use accurate, updated data and analytics to determine your future workforce and workplace models.
4 Build deeper career-management competency among your managers.

Table 5.1: The Five Myths, Underlying Needs, and New Realities

Myth	Underlying needs	Undiscovered new realities
Older workers cost too much	• Need to know your real costs at a granular level and in your workforce model • Need to rethink ageist policies • Need to present new, smart career options that work for the organization and the employee • Need to foster manager-employee discussions that establish relationships to avoid defaulting into legal "dos and don'ts" • Need to ensure you do not perpetuate arrangements that no longer work	• Older workers cost less than expected • New models present excellent value-for-money options
Training older workers is a cost, not an investment	• Need to base resource allocation and career paths on real data • Need employee and management training programs to be based on new career time line realities • Need updated approaches to culture-building programs that reject 1930s thinking	• Lifelong learning programs integrate employees of all ages to the benefit of the entire organization • Older workers thrive with new training opportunities
Employees have a best before date	• Need a talent structure that doesn't reinforce 1930s thinking • Need an approach that recognizes that career change occurs at different times and different reasons for everyone – not based on chronological age	• Ability to contribute value (not chronological age) drives workforce policy and decisions

Myth	Underlying needs	Undiscovered new realities
	• Need a way to plan for future workforce change in a way that can be predicted • Need meaningful training and career development to continue throughout working life • Need employees and managers to consider work and life interests as well as salary when discussing future opportunities • Need to address decline and agedness separately from "aging"	
Older workers are less productive than younger ones	• Need to establish reliable methods and metrics for data collection • Need to provide flexible options for the improvement of productivity	• Older workers thrive with new training opportunities • Older workers may choose lateral moves or change of direction to reenergize and produce peak productivity levels
Performance management is different for older workers	• Need to identify the cause of performance issues, not assume they are a result of age • Need to value age diversity and become aware of inherent ageism • Need programs that build an intergenerational culture • Need to ensure employees of all ages are challenged and growing • Need to address performance issues quickly with any employee, regardless of age	• High performance expectations are in place for all employees and supported by all managers

The quick fix is simply to be conscious of the myth under which you are operating. But to capitalize on what you've discovered, you'll need to do a good deal more. We'll begin the process of discovery and solution-building by first exploring the five myths. In part 3, we'll continue this process by providing a roadmap to help you chart a new course that builds on the four action areas described above. Table 5.2 will help you identify which issues are at play in

Table 5.2: Identifying the Myths at Play in Your Organization

Myth	Not an issue	Might be an issue	Is an issue
Money myths			
Peak performance myths			

your organization so you can structure an intervention. Use the guide of suggested interventions below to help you prioritize the subjects you will address.

Suggested Interventions for Myths That *Are Not* an Issue:
- Educate your leadership team about the myth and expose indicators that the myth is at work in your organization.
- At least once every quarter, ask testing questions to see if this myth has crept into managers' or employees' thinking.

Suggested Interventions for Myths That *Might Be* an Issue:
- Ask questions to discover if it is an issue.
- Identify two or three leaders to frame the issue and set out measures that help you determine the impact this myth is having on your business.

Suggested Interventions for Myths That *Are* an Issue:
- Identify two or three leaders to frame the issue and set out measures to help you determine the impact this myth is having on your business.
- Focus on the underlying needs that cause the myth to be accepted as a business objection.
- Map the needs against the five identified themes to identify focus areas.
- Schedule a meeting or retreat with executives and other leaders to tackle the relevant theme(s) using data and creative facilitation techniques such as design thinking. Imagine what would be different if this myth were not at play in your organization.

6

MONEY MYTHS

While it is generally considered wise to aim for reduced costs and improved profits, if you are like many of the organizational leaders with whom we've worked, your metrics may be faulty and your results seriously skewed, based as they are on outdated or erroneous assumptions and expectations. It is entirely possible that you are using the same standards and measurements you have relied on for years – systems that fail to account for today's workforce transformations.

Without data supporting their belief that older workers are more costly than other segments of the workforce, many leaders accept the "money myths" as absolute truths. But embracing unfounded beliefs is more than foolish. It is bad business. Faulty premises lead to poor decisions – decisions that may affect morale, productivity, and the bottom line. Merely comparing hourly or yearly salaries is imprudent because it fails to account for added value. Still, the myths about older workers being disproportionately costly persist. Here, we explode two pervasive myths that may be costing your company a great deal more than you realize.

The Myth of Excessive Salaries

Everyone knows that older workers cost too much. Raise the subject among headhunters or HR specialists and you'll hear that assertion so often it's like standing in an echo chamber. And because it is generally thought that the costs associated with older workers are unreasonably high, current wisdom holds that it is good strategy to replace older workers with younger workers based on the economics of lower salaries and scaled-back pension and benefits packages. Furthermore, since companies think older workers cost more in salaries and benefits, and are less productive than younger ones, there is an inclination to disincentivize older workers or remove them from the payroll completely.

The Reality

Typically, people who have been working for decades earn salaries and benefits that are costlier than newer hires. But data going back decades indicates that an employee's earning potential is maximized by their early forties (Guvenen et al. 2015). It is a grave mistake to compare the dollars per hour earned by older and younger workers without inserting the relevant calculations for the costs of onboarding, training, time-to-productivity, replacement, and so on. The hard truth is that in the long run, older, more experienced workers may actually cost a company about the same or a good deal less than their younger counterparts. In a practical guide published by the American Management Association, W. Rothwell and his coauthors reminds managers that, "while workers with tenure are entitled to more vacation time and pension costs related to number of years worked, replacing workers is not cost free" (Rothwell et al. 2008, 43). In fact, the factors associated with onboarding and orienting new staff often costs up to an additional 93 percent of the employee's first-year salary (Rothwell et al. 2008).

Observations from the Field

Robert was the president of the Canadian division of a global toy manufacturer headquartered in the United States. The Canadian operation employed five thousand people and maintained a cost structure in which labor costs contributed between 4 and 6 percent of overall direct costs, while the American operation ran at 20 percent.

After months of discussion, Robert was dismayed that he was unable to convince headquarters to reverse a decision to move production from Canada to Latin America, where hourly labor rates were admittedly lower, but where manufacturing quality would decrease and transportation and other costs would increase.

The plant was closed and its operations shifted south. The desired cost savings were never realized and Robert left the company. Now well into his own Legacy Career, Robert notes that this was a situation where the company had the data but failed to use it. In the case of the aging workforce, he asserts, the data isn't even a part of the discussion because the real costs of the aging workforce are unknown and undervalued.

Research also shows that older workers take less time off than their younger counterparts, often because they have no child-care responsibilities (Rudgard 2015). Plus, they tend to have fewer injuries because they've learned how to minimize risks. But when it comes to older workers, facts do not influence strategy as much as they should. We may be living in a time of fake news and made-up facts, but if we are to lead the world in business, creativity, productivity, and profits, we can't allow assumptions, stereotypes, and myths to pass for truth, unchecked and unchallenged. And right now it seems that the belief that an older worker is more expensive than a younger one trumps all evidence to the contrary.

In a review of case law in the United States, and the United Kingdom, Pnina Alon-Shenker finds that American and British employees have few protections against nonhiring or dismissal when it is supported by a cost rationale. She provides many examples where cost justification was weak or nonexistent. So it seems that the courts in the United States and the United Kingdom accept that employers are justified in shedding older workers based on their supposed cost, even when research and evidence indicates that there is no clear cost burden in most cases. However, Alon-Shenker asserts that while it is probable that courts will continue to agree that employers can use cost as justification for nonhiring or for dismissal, the issue is further complicated by the requirement that such decisions conform to human rights codes, which prohibit cost determinations founded on age-based stereotypes (Alon-Shenker 2014). Here facts matter. Employers may make the case that older workers are more expensive, but courts are required to assess this claim to ensure that it is based on complete and verifiable information.

Incidentally, a quick Internet search for a reliable formula to estimate the real costs of employees yielded 11,300,000 results, many of them offering free and easy cost calculators. We scanned the first 50 on the list, and while all considered direct costs like taxes, benefits, and administration, and some included indirect costs such as office facilities and transportation, not a single formula allowed for the value of experience or expertise. Nor did they factor in the cost

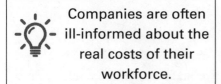

Companies are often ill-informed about the real costs of their workforce.

of retention or turnover. Since big companies usually use dedicated software and a team of accountants to calculate costs, we wonder if either considers new workplace demographics and employee value versus expenses in calculating the real costs of employees on the payroll.

While the research comparing the stereotypical qualities of younger versus older workers is limited, our clients report that older workers are more punctual, more reliable, take less time off, and are less likely to quit after investments have been made in their development. This appraisal is supported by the few studies that have come to light (Van Dalen, Henkens, and Schippers 2010). Moreover, mature workers require less training, less supervision, and often produce a higher-quality product, which, in itself, has positive financial effects (Families and Work Institute n.d.). Furthermore, our client work leads us to conclude that salary is not the most important

Observations from the Field

Charles publishes a small-town newspaper known for quality reporting and exceptional writing. Indeed, since its inception six years ago, the paper has won several awards. Much of this success is due to Jeff, the paper's talented editor-in-chief.

When Jeff accepted a job at a big-city paper, Charles understood and wished him well, then began a search for Jeff's replacement. After months of reading dozens of poorly written résumés, Charles finally hired Nancy, the best of the bunch – a recent journalism grad who demonstrated a good deal of enthusiasm and a willingness to learn.

It quickly became clear that Nancy was not up to the job. While she'd graduated from journalism school, she had failed to master grammar and punctuation – essential skills for the paper. Equally troubling for an editor-in-chief, Nancy didn't know how to structure a news story. Worse still, she lacked the experience and judgment to decide which stories would be most important to local residents, so she often overlooked or buried what should have been lead stories.

Charles turned to Lebo for help, and after assessing Nancy's skills, Lebo suggested that ongoing remedial help would be necessary if Charles wanted Nancy to grow into her current role. Charles took the advice and hired a retired journalism professor to tutor Nancy twice a week.

Charles continued to pay Nancy her full salary and he paid her tutor as well – while Charles was compelled to do most of Nancy's work himself. And although Nancy's skills slowly improved, it soon became clear she was years away from attaining the competency she needed for the job.

After eight months, Nancy quit. It was a costly experience for all involved – emotionally and financially – and Charles insists he'll hire only seasoned editors from now on.

career driver for mature employees, who are often willing to work for significantly less to shift into the Legacy Career they want.

Human resource experts contend it's a mistake to assume that older workers cost more in benefits and are less productive than younger workers. "Both concerns are untrue. While older workers may take longer to recover from injuries, studies show that they use fewer sick days on the whole than their younger counterparts," says management professor Peter Cappelli, who directs the Wharton Center for Human Resources at the University of Pennsylvania (quoted in Knowledge@Wharton 2010). Health-care costs are actually less for older workers, according to Cappelli, because most no longer have small children as dependents on their health-care plans. American workers also become eligible for Medicare at age sixty-five, which can further reduce an employer's health-care bills (Knowledge@Wharton 2010). Health-care costs are not an issue for Canadians, and an Australian study comparing the costs of younger and older workers comes to a similar conclusion, ultimately supporting an investment in older workers (Brooke 2003).

In an online paper, the AARP also quotes Professor Cappelli, who it says "has looked more closely at these stereotypes, pulling together research from fields like economics, demography and psychology" (Reade 2013). Says Cappelli: "Every aspect of job performance gets better as we age ... The juxtaposition between the superior performance of older workers and the discrimination against them in the workplace just really makes no sense" (quoted in Reade 2013).

Studies show that older workers are not more expensive.

It is also worth noting that a study completed by the Canadian government's Seniors Secretariat revealed that employers across the country were convinced their employees over fifty preferred to stay in the same roles at the same salary for as long as they continued working. But as we have found in our own work, when researchers surveyed and interviewed these very same workers, they were shocked to discover that assumption to be false (Carstairs and Keon 2009).

A majority of respondents said they want improved life-work balance and would be happy to trade a portion of their salary for the opportunity to manage fewer people, attend fewer meetings, and have more flexibility in scheduling and working hours. Analysis of the study's findings clearly exposed employers' lack of understanding about the interests, abilities, and potential contribution of older workers – a lack of understanding that caused employers to assume restrictions and limitations that did not exist.

Observations from the Field

The employers' dilemma with this information involves their concerns about constructive dismissal claims. If companies offer roles with lower salary and limited span of control to mature employees, they fear these workers could bring a constructive dismissal claim against them, despite purporting to want this very arrangement. It is a real cause for concern because of the potential financial consequences.

Alon-Shenker (2014) points out that in other human rights areas, employers are required to demonstrate that alternatives were provided, and that discriminatory decisions were not made based on a protected characteristic. In the case of older workers, where the employer believes that age equates to increased cost, would the same test hold? Put another way, if the employer presents only lower-cost positions, how can that employer defend against claims of constructive dismissal?

This myth – the mistaken belief that older workers cost more than younger ones – may well be the single greatest impediment to intergenerational workforces and workplaces that capitalize on our ability to be productive well past the age of sixty-five. Employers are trapped, unable to offer innovative career paths, because these new avenues may actually embody the definition of constructive dismissal.

As unenlightened as their employers, many mature workers think their only career options are to continue doing the senior-level position they currently occupy, or to quit their job and take a front-line retail position in a company that values mature, experienced, or retired employees as a special asset and a competitive advantage. It's a foolish belief that seems to be rooted in archaic workplace structures or outdated career-path routes. Of course, those are not the only options available to older workers, nor do those options make the best use of employer salary and benefit dollars.

Costs soar, not because older workers remain in the workforce, but because they are disengaged, stuck, underused, and marginal-ized – all this because there is an unfounded belief that they are expensive. The issue is not that they cost more per hour than a younger employee might, or that they are costly assets. The issue, rather, is that their equity is being poorly invested.

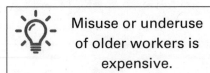

Misuse or underuse of older workers is expensive.

Key Points

- When calculating employee costs, move beyond simple wage comparisons to include calculations for the costs of onboarding, training, time-to-productivity, replacement, and so forth. Con-sider the inestimable value of wisdom, experience, and loyalty.
- Consider offering work-life balance "benefits" as alternatives for older workers.
- De-marginalize older workers and receive concomitant value for dollars invested.
- Reconsider how new approaches to career ownership might empower older workers to create or find appealing new roles within your organization without triggering constructive dis-missal claims.

The Myth of Squandered Budgets

It is widely believed that training older workers is a cost not an in-vestment. Put another way, management has long considered it a waste of money to bother training the mature employees on the payroll. It is a firmly fixed idea based on a number of erroneous assumptions, including:

- Mature workers are too old to learn.
- Even if they could learn, they'll soon retire, so any ROI would be short-lived.
- Mature workers have no interest in training and development.

We often hear employers say some version of the following: "Lisa, if we have a limited budget to allocate to training, development, and career-related programs, why wouldn't I allocate those precious dollars to our youngest and newest employees? Why would I spend that money on the population that has received the most training over their lifetime and is the most likely to leave in the next few years?"

Why, indeed? In tough business environments, training and career-management activities are often reprioritized as useful but not urgent activities. It seems logical that new employees need the biggest chunk of development dollars as they enter and adjust to your workplace. They are the ones who are most malleable, trainable, and energetic, aren't they?

It's equally logical to assume that more experienced staff actually require fewer hours of career-management or training programs, especially when management is typically blind to today's shifting career time lines and may be completely unaware that these programs could be of significant value to employees at any age or stage. It's not that managers deliberately disregard older workers; it's a function of the downward pressure to focus time, energy, and capital on the youngest generation entering the workplace. As is so often the case, logic, not facts, drives business leaders to believe there is a greater ROI on programs for new graduates and younger workers than for older ones. Since younger employees are seen as the future of the business and the purveyors of the magic, programs for these employees are considered investments in the future.

Companies use metrics like increased new-graduate-hire retention (past the first twenty-four months) and faster time-to-job productivity to prove the value of these programs. Conversely, companies rarely include mature employees in training programs, nor do they measure the ROI for the few older employees who may find a way to slip in. While there is still no universal definition for "older worker," management generally assumes that the costs of training and development for mature employees far outweigh the benefits (McCarthy et al. 2014). But a 2015 report prepared for the AARP by Aon Hewitt (2015) debunks this kind of thinking by explaining that characteristics commonly found in employees that are fifty or older – such as professionalism, strong work ethic, knowledge, and reliability – make them ideal employees who should be included in all available opportunities because it is likely to pay off in a number of unexpected ways.

Of course, excluding older workers from training and development opportunities sets them up as employees who don't keep up, thereby reinforcing ageist stereotypes. They become unfortunately conspicuous – relying on yesterday's technologies, styles, and points of view.

Observations from the Field

In twenty-two years of delivering skill-building communications workshops to Fortune 500 clients, Lebo rarely met an employee over fifty – not because they didn't want to attend, but because they were not invited to attend. On those occasions when a mature employee asked for special permission from their employer to take the training, they seldom received it. Yet without exception, every older employee who was lucky enough to somehow receive approval and slip into the program rated it five out of five in terms of "value to my work."

Vince was the manager of a highly skilled sales team selling big-ticket medical devices. Vince had attended Lebo's sales presentation course, liked what he learned, and saw it as an essential tool for his whole team. He had tried twice to send team members to the program but on both occasions his VP scratched the names of mature team members off the list.

Still, Vince was determined, and since he wanted everyone to attend, he scheduled a session at his local headquarters so he could avoid explanations about training dollars. It was the only way, he said, to be sure that everyone could get the training they deserved.

Following the workshop, Vince sent a thank-you note to Lebo. "You gave us the skills we need to beat the competition," he wrote, "and you gave us a common language, which I think is just as important. Everyone said it was a great team-building opportunity but what surprised me is that my most senior people gave the course the highest scores."

The Reality

There are a few truths to acknowledge here.

Special programs are always a cost if you consider your employees as assets that depreciate in value over time. They are an investment only when you think of employees as talent equity whose value increases with experience and education. Indeed, equity investments pay off for those employees' entire working lives – whether they have moved elsewhere or not. We address talent equity as a framework in more detail in chapter 10.

Then, too, workforce-related programs, including training for any demographic, frequently offer a weak ROI, and because they do, they must always be carefully vetted, designed for purpose, and allocated to the specific populations where they are most likely to have an impact. At first blush, it appears that training for skill-building and company culture orientation will surely help retain more millennials who complain they are overlooked for lack of skills and who feel compelled to quit to pursue other, more fulfilling opportunities. According to Deloitte's 2016 Millennial Survey, "Forty-four percent of Millennials say, if given the choice, they would like to leave their current employers in the next two years. A perceived lack of leadership-skill development and feelings of being overlooked are compounded by larger issues around work/life balance, the desire for flexibility, and a conflict of values" (Deloitte Touche Tohmatsu 2016). Based on these findings, it seems logical that training dollars and workforce program efforts should target this critical population. But the logic is based on a hunch and an incomplete understanding of workforce trends – and the logic is faulty.

In December 2015 more than 3 million Americans quit their jobs, the highest number in more than nine years (Kitroeff 2016). As noted above, the US Bureau of Labor Statistics (2016) reported that as of September 2016 that employees' average tenure with a company in the United States had declined to 4.3 years for men and 4.0 years for women. Some of the decline is attributed to the increase in younger workers entering the workforce. Yes, millennials are a big population. In Canada, millennials have surpassed boomers as the biggest cohort in the workforce, and the Pew Research Center reports that, according to the latest US census, "Millennials have surpassed Baby Boomers as the nation's largest living generation." That said, retention rates across all age groups are on the decline, obliging many economists and leaders to ponder the *Bloomberg* headline, "Have Millennials made quitting more common?" (Kitroeff 2016).

You need engagement strategies for employees of all ages – strategies that integrate the generations. After all, they are working together and influencing each other every day.

Observations from the Field

A perplexed executive from an engineering company phoned Taylor to report that one of his top senior leaders (we'll call him Bob) had just surprised him by tendering his resignation. At the age of fifty-four, Bob had determined he'd saved sufficient funds to confidently leave his job. He had no offer elsewhere and reported no plan to seek a new position. Only the week before, the executive had considered Bob a top succession candidate who could take on C-level responsibility over the next three to five years.

At his exit interview, Bob expressed no specific concerns about the company or his job. In fact, he specifically said how much he'd enjoyed his work. He was simply ready to change the balance of work and life. He also expressed a desire for growth, since he'd been in the same industry for many years.

The executive and many of the company's staff struggled to understand how Bob could make such a decision. How could a senior leader walk away from a job he enjoyed and do … nothing? But, of course, Bob didn't do "nothing." He traveled and spent time with his now grown children. He signed up for an interesting course, and nine months later began working as a freelancer with start-ups in high growth stages, helping them manage the growth they were experiencing.

Ironically, six months after Bob left, the engineering company opened a new division focused on early-stage entrepreneurial companies. Bob has no regrets about leaving the company and he loves his new freelance-focused Legacy Career. But the company deeply regrets Bob's departure and the unsettling impact it had on its other employees.

Your workforce is a symbiotic ecosystem in which all generations must work together synergistically. The ability to achieve the goal of any program – whether it be to increase productivity, enhance retention, develop skills, or whatever – depends on how well the individual employee integrates his or her learning into the organization's ecosystem. Too many companies invest heavily in programs that target onboarding and retaining new graduates only to discover at the end of the honeymoon period (typically twelve months) that these employees demonstrate no stronger company loyalty than do the employees of competitors without such programs. One reason for the lack of long-term staying power can be summed up in the now infamous Peter Drucker quote, "Culture eats strategy for breakfast."

How many organizations have mentoring programs as part of new graduate and high potential leadership programs, but fail to train the mentors? Strategic workforce programs that target a specific population but fail to align with the overall culture of the organization are doomed to bomb. When you invest in new-graduate development at the exclusion of other demographic groups, you are making it perfectly clear that you favor younger employees while being sublimely indifferent to your most loyal employees. What's more, you create an artificial environment throughout the program that is at odds with the day in, day out culture in which your staff is immersed. Is it any wonder older employees become disengaged?

Long-term employees have outlived any special attention and instead become examples of career stagnation. It's obvious to everyone that younger employees are preferred as generations are pitted against each other. It's also clear that your organization is not a place where one wants to "get old." As a result, career paths are decided with an eye on the right time to exit before the "us" of today (younger workers) becomes the "them" of tomorrow (older workers). This rigid divide infuses every aspect of your working culture, and programs intended for team-building or for bringing the generations together feel artificial or forced to the people attending them. There's strain between getting everyday work done and participating in special programs designed to transfer knowledge and context from old to young. In many cases, these programs are cast with hopeful or ironic titles like "reverse mentoring" in an attempt to convey the sentiment that everyone benefits from the relationship, that there is a give and a get for both parties. But the ROI is difficult to measure and the actual experience often falls short of the intended goal.

There's another truth worth acknowledging here. Given the speed at which technology is changing, and recognizing the realities of a lengthened work life, it is almost certain that any given technology will be obsolete long before a mature worker actually retires.

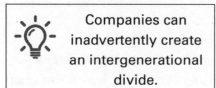

Companies can inadvertently create an intergenerational divide.

So here's the real truth. Workforce programs that are not well designed, or those that grow out of anecdotal evidence, assumptions, suppositions, or myths, are extremely costly; they expend time, consume funds, and can lead to a slow deterioration of culture. They can inadvertently demotivate older workers while theoretically intending to convince them they are held in high esteem. If your company is focused on loyalty, career management, lifelong learning, and a culture of intergenerational collaboration, segmenting your programs by age is not just counterproductive, it's downright dangerous.

When you think about the talent escalator described in chapter 4 and consider the impact of the Legacy Career phase, it's clear that if your workforce is to function as an integrated system, people on the upper steps need opportunities to keep moving, to grow, and to see where their future is heading as much as people on the lower steps need to understand what's above them. In fact, here's where the linear nature of the escalator analogy starts to be seriously problematic. In today's workplaces, segmenting development programs and opportunities by age creates an artificial career message that does not align with today's world of work. Today's world is changing so rapidly that older workers are looking for opportunities to grow and expand as they begin to seek their own Legacy Career path, and it's important to remember that these employees are your strongest brand ambassadors, trainers, and keepers of your culture. Whether they stay with you or leave, they are a critical part of your long-term success. Investing in these members of your organization will pay far greater dividends than spot training programs for younger workers – especially if their training doesn't align with a career culture that insists on placing an expiry date on usefulness.

Key Points

- Use good data. It's essential to use workforce models that are clear and measurable to evaluate current results and project future outcomes.
- Understand your workplace demographics and analyze trends through multiple lenses to be sure you are identifying the root causes of an issue, not merely addressing its symptoms.
- Take an intergenerational approach to your workforce programs. Age is not a business driver. Identify the underlying business need or issue that all generations can help address.
- Recognize that corporate culture and values drive behavior, program adoption, and the ROI you can expect to realize.
- Don't overlook employees of any age when offering training and development. It is costly to do so and it impacts the effectiveness and productivity of all staff. It also marks your employer brand and demotivates your most loyal employees.
- Be suspicious of the assumption that experienced staff has fewer developmental needs than younger employees. While they may not need the same type of training as younger staff, staying current, relevant, and active in the workforce community is critical for personal and business success. If your workforce is out of date and disconnected, your lack of investment in this area is likely a cause.

- Avoid creating artificial programs that remove people from their everyday roles. Infuse development opportunities into everyday work so cross-functional teams with members of all ages who work together every day can support each other's growth and development while addressing real business situations.
- Avoid the trap of assuming that boomers' only value is as mentors or custodians of knowledge. Longevity does not automatically make someone a good mentor. But if mentoring is an integral part of your company's workforce strategy, mentorship training is advisable.

7

PEAK PERFORMANCE MYTHS

Irrespective of the business you are in, maximizing workforce performance is a perpetual goal. Great effort, substantial time, and significant dollars are expended to achieve it. But one sector of the workforce is usually at a disadvantage from the get-go – older workers. In most organizations, there is a firmly held belief that older workers are past their prime and either cannot or will not ever again perform at levels equivalent to the younger workers on the payroll. Often, this belief is based on an anecdote about one employee who failed to perform and who, it is thought, represents the entire cohort. But this is a myth that often leads to poor workforce planning strategies. Still, it is a belief as solidly stuck as a barnacle. In this chapter we tackle three such myths about older workers and the truth about peak performance – because discovering the truth leads to high-performing organizations.

The Myth of the "Best Before Date"

In our society, there is an assumption that employees have a limited shelf life. There is a common belief that employees reach the end of their "working life expectancy" at around age sixty or sixty-five, when they'll have reached their time limit on productivity and general usefulness. And while sixty-five has long been considered the norm for a worker's best before date, age-based limitations perpetuate ageism and ageist policies in ways that no longer serve either the individual or the organization.

The Reality

Setting an age limit on any individual's ability to meaningfully contribute in the workplace is a mistake today, and perhaps always was. In 1935, when the average life expectancy was sixty-two, the United States enacted Social Security and introduced a retirement age intended to ensure that workers nearing the end of their natural life had the support they needed to step away from work and tend to their declining health. Today, the statistics portal Statista reports that average life expectancy in North America has reached eighty-one (Stastista 2016). But work-life expectancy is still stuck in 1935. If we hold on to sixty-five as a reasonable retirement age, we fail to understand that the structures, lifestyle, and nature of work are very different today than they were decades ago, when retirement was first contemplated and sixty-two was the average age of death.

Pension eligibility may not align with an employee's time line for exiting the workforce.

As governments around the world struggle to redefine pension and benefits eligibility ages, it's easy to mistake these policy discussions about age for a decisive answer to the question of when to retire. But this would be a miscalculation.

In their book *The 100 Year Life*, Gratton and Scott (2016) explain that increased lifespans have obliterated the practicality of the three-stage life – an archaic view that divides a lifetime into education, work, and retirement. Gratton and Scott talk about the emergence of "age agnostic" activities and multifaceted, multistaged careers. And while sixty-five remains a common benchmark, that standard is irrational when you consider what it means to the individuals who may have another twenty or thirty healthy and active years ahead of them, as well as to the companies who are oblivious to the rich source of talent slipping out the door.

Observations from the Field

Sue had been working in a Boston elementary school as a school psychologist for forty-three years. As retirement neared, she knew she'd have a healthy pension and needed no additional income. But she was an active, energetic woman who thrived on intellectual challenge and she simply wasn't ready to give it all up.

Still, Sue was tired of the bureaucracy and politics. She looked for a way to transfer her skills within the public school system, but what she found only reinforced what she already knew – that the system was rigid, uncompromising, and uncreative; that there was nothing "different" available for her to do; that she could stay on staff for as long as she chose, but that they'd rather see her leave than try something new. After much contemplation, Sue reluctantly retired.

Then Sue discovered an association working with socially dysfunctional young adults. She signed up as a volunteer and spent a few months getting a feel for what was going on. Soon, she offered to become a personal coach to young people setting out in the world. Shortly after that, she suggested that an innovative grandparents support group might be an excellent complement to programs already on the schedule. It was – and it filled quickly.

The association was thrilled to accept Sue's offer of time and expertise and she now works three days a week using her highly refined skills in a completely new arena. Some of her work is paid; some is volunteer. At this point Sue has been happily involved with the association for four years and has no plans to "retire" any time soon. She considers her income irrelevant and she loves the work she's doing, but her decision to move on and transfer her skills was a real loss to the school board for which she worked for forty-three years.

The suggestion that workers are racing against a specific best before date is valid only if the work involved requires a specific skill or ability that declines over time (Fisher, Chaffee, and Sonnega 2016). And even then, it is not uniformly true that at a specific age functional decline occurs. Intensely physical jobs, work requiring exceptionally dexterous small motor skills, or work demanding extreme intellectual agility might fall into this category – although aging is only one of several factors that can limit an individual's ability to continue in these roles. The research shows that people with more education work longer, and while that may be a chicken-and-egg scenario, even when considering physical labor or intellectual work, we can't assume that everyone ages out at precisely the same age or stage (Munnell 2015).

While we don't advocate age limits on workplace and community contribution, we recognize that the fixation on age stems from significant workforce realities. First, physical and mental decline can impact an individual's ability to or interest in pursuing specific roles. However, the rate and extent of these physiological changes are different for each person. Furthermore, they are not tied to a specific chronological age, tend to occur much later than they once did, and can be impacted by many factors. Whether or not a particular role requires a specific skill, it is bad policy to assume that age is the single and definitive limiting factor on who can or cannot complete the work. Sometimes it's a lack of up-to-the-minute skills.

One of the unintended consequences of this age-based expectation is the withdrawal of training. For all other ages, training is recognized as a tool to engage and enhance performance. It is used to ensure that employees remain productive, responsive to the shifting nature of work, and at the top of their field. But tighter budgets and assumptions about future engagement leave older workers out of training programs, thereby setting up the conditions for these workers to see their skills become dated, and because they are, reinforcing unfair stereotypes. Somewhere in this exclusion from training is buried a number of ageist clichés, such as older employees are not interested in learning new skills, or "you can't teach an old dog new tricks."

A second negative dimension to the best before date fallacy is based on the assumption that, if older workers remain, they stand in the way of younger generations trying to enter the workforce or to move up into more senior roles. The "Lump of Labor Fallacy" described in chapter 4 assumes a finite number of jobs within the economy and simple if devastating consequences: younger workers can enter the workforce only if someone currently holding a job leaves.

Economists have argued for decades that this is untrue and studies show that OECD countries that have increased participation of older workers in the labor force, youth employment also increases. Historically, whether it's a white- or blue-collar job, senior or skilled workers routinely generate work for less experienced workers.

On the other hand, if older workers continue to be undervalued, underchallenged, and underused, they may indeed clog the system while simply treading the top step of the escalator. Keep in mind the two main assumptions that underlie the lump of labor belief:

1 That older workers want to continue in exactly the same roles they currently hold
2 That older workers value their current salary level more than they value changes in responsibility or a more flexible work-life balance.

Observations from the Field

Paul has worked as an architect for more than forty-five years, and he is well respected in his field across North America. Now, at age seventy-one, his work is as important to him as ever. He takes pride in his profession and feels strongly that he is an important player in the client work he does and in helping his company to train and guide new architects coming up in the industry.

The company Paul works for structures its architects and engineers into customer-facing practices, with each employee having specific targets for billable hours. Paul has not met his target for more than five years. While there is widespread recognition that Paul contributes significantly to the firm, there is concern that he is not meeting core metrics and is still receiving full compensation. If he were younger, long ago managers would have had performance-management conversations with Paul and challenged his fitness to continue to work in the department.

Paul knows he has challenges in meeting his billable-hour target. Most projects require significant travel and he finds the pace, time zone changes, and eighteen-hour workdays exhausting. He also completes his work using tools and technologies with which he is comfortable, tools that are often different from the software packages his younger colleagues use. He is annoyed that colleagues refer to him as technically challenged because it isn't that he can't learn new technology or that he hasn't embraced new social media tools in his private life – it's that he hasn't received formal training on any of the new technologies, so he uses the traditional approaches he has mastered, knowing they serve him well for the work the needs to do.

Financially, Paul has limited resources, and he is worried that he hasn't saved enough for retirement so he can't stop working altogether. But, he has not consulted a financial planner and has only a vague idea of how much he and his wife need to live the lifestyle they are hoping to live. He comes from a family where most live well past ninety and he expects to do the same. He is also seriously invested in his work. He believes he is a pioneer in the industry and his peers and colleagues readily agree, calling him, "a giant in the field." Being held in esteem is very important to Paul.

When Taylor first spoke with Paul he had a sense of how many more years he wanted to continue in his current role, asserting that his only options were to continue doing what he was doing or quit the firm and work as a frontline customer service representative at a local hardware store.

Management at Paul's company was in a quandary about what to do next. Their ideal scenario was that somehow Paul could remain part of the company in a role where he could meet the requirements of the position he held. However, management felt a job shift might imply a demotion or salary decrease, since the highest-paid positions in the organization were roles tied to billable hours, especially at a senior level. Management turned to Challenge Factory to see how challenging outdated career thinking might provide new solutions that obliterated the assumptions preventing leadership from finding solutions on their own.

It's a question of mindset. After decades of career experience inside organizations that provide employees with career paths and development programs, it is logical for employees to expect their employer to define what is possible in the later stages of their career. They are accustomed to taking cues from their company rather than striking out on their own. Without cues, employees assume that no next steps are available to them. With options, employees make suitable choices for a meaningful and productive Legacy Career. Smart organizations expect career ownership from every employee at every age and stage, and they provide appropriate tools to support older employees as they transition with purpose. At the same time, transitioning employees need assistance to explore talents, needs, passions, and impact for new opportunities to maximize growth, engagement, and relevance. Then, too, frontline managers need help to recognize the demographic realities of today's workforce and to understand why it is a big mistake to count boomers out.

Key Points

- Expect career ownership from every employee at every age and stage.

- Provide tools that support transition with purpose, ensuring employees explore talents, needs, passions, and impact for other opportunities within the company.
- Rethink roles within your company to capitalize on what's been called the longevity dividend.
- Educate frontline managers about the demographic realities of the workforce and provide reasons why it's a big mistake to count boomers out.

The Myth of Diminished Productivity

Older workers are less productive than younger workers. It's well known that older workers are slower, less motivated, and less energetic than younger employees, all of which makes them less productive than their younger counterparts – at least that's the common wisdom. Indeed, it is a belief so firmly held in the workplace that it affects hiring practices as well as performance reviews, salaries, and career-path opportunities. And to add insult to injury, the lower an older worker is in the workplace hierarchy, the less productive he or she is seen to be (Van Dalen, Henkens, and Schippers 2010).

The Reality

It turns out that productivity is more a case of attitude than age, and interestingly, it's the attitude of the employer that carries the most weight (Van Dalen, Henkens, and Schippers 2010).

Research shows that whether or not older workers are considered less productive than their younger coworkers has a good deal more to do with perception than with reality. And the most important perception in righting this equation rests with the employer. In their study of older workers in retail settings, James, McKechnie, and

Swanberg highlight that relationships with immediate supervisors have the most profound impact on employee engagement (James, McKechnie, and Swanberg 2011).

The truth is that productivity is not inversely correlated with age. Whether an older worker is perceived to be productive – or not – depends more on the employee's age and position in the hierarchy. That is, the higher the position of the employee, the more productive that employee is perceived to be. Furthermore, there is an unfounded belief that productivity is inevitably reduced in older workers because they are burdened with failing health, decreased physical energy, and higher rates of absenteeism than their younger counterparts (Robertson and Tracy 1998).

But research reveals that some aspects of cognitive functioning decline as early as our twenties and thirties. Indeed, when asked about improving brain health for young workers, Dr. Nasreen Khatri, a neuroscientist with the Rotman Research Institute, said that "when it comes to good brain health habits, the best time to start is yesterday" (quoted in Pearce 2017). The impact of aging on productivity is not predetermined; there are other factors to consider in addition to chronological age.

> The perception of decreased productivity turns on the attitude of the employer, not the actual output of the employee.

Engagement in later-life careers is a big topic, and one for which we provided a foundation in part 1 of this book. The research in this area is astonishingly rich, demonstrating repeatedly that all of these assumptions are patently false and that the perception of decreased productivity is simply dead wrong – and yet the perception persists. It seems that stereotyping older workers based on psychological mechanisms could be described as standard practice – influencing the way managers treat older employees and the way older workers must confront barriers that others do not (Henkens 2005).

In a 2009 European study, it was noted that job involvement is a critical condition to ensure continued engagement, as well as a potential indicator of productivity (Buyens et al. 2009). Older workers who are no longer engaged in career-management activities (including at least annual future-facing discussions, ongoing learning-goal identification, and support for developing new skills and networks) feel invisible to the organization. This invisibility begins to be a self-fulfilling prophecy. Many organizations have mechanisms to measure who in the work-force is part of a high-potential cohort or a high-performance cohort.

But our discussions with clients lead us to note that many of these structures filter employees, if not by age, then by years of service. As part of developing the "next generation" of leaders and employees, employers are closely tracking the productivity and impact of work-ers in their early and mid-careers. The tracking that is consistently applied to employees in the Legacy Career phase is related to their costs. But, without an understanding of the impact of the individu-al's work, costs alone are only one side of the equation. Organiza-tional network theory suggests that there are critical nodes within any organization. These employees are highly networked. They are seen as culture-keepers and their beliefs carry an incredible amount of weight. Their influence on other team members' performance and productivity is immense and often underestimated. Because the world of work is in flux today and is behaving like a social move-ment (as outlined in chapter 1) it is relevant to note that nodes within networks have the ability to mobilize, empower, and promote col-lective action and alternative cultural practice (Diani 2015). Inside today's organizations, boomers are being selected as mentors across organizations because of their experience, institutional knowledge, and awareness of organizational culture. But their informal role as the network's key nodes – influencers of the entire workforce's pro-ductivity and morale – is frequently overlooked. Often it takes one of these key actors to either leave the organization or to direct their network's energy to counterproductive activities before management recognizes their real influence.

The truth is that with the wisdom, polished skills, improved accuracy, and judgment born of experience and practice, mature workers' productivity may well exceed that of younger employees, and indeed often does. Several recent studies show that "older workers are, in fact, worthy of their pay, in the sense that their contribution to firm-level productivity exceeds their contribution to the wage bill" (Cardoso, Guimarães, and Varejão 2011). It's also worth noting that employees are often perceived to be more productive if they are masters of the hard skills, not the soft ones – and it is the soft skills at which mature workers so often excel. But "both employers and employees, young and old, view hard skills as far more important than soft skills" (Van Dalen, Henkens, and Schippers 2010).

It is essential here to appreciate the need for a psychological reset to ensure that older workers are seen as the individuals they are, not as clichés or stereotypes viewed through a lens clouded by misperception and myth. Assumptions that link age to productivity are unfounded, and treating an entire cohort as less productive because of their age is an explicit example of ageism in the workplace. Every individual is unique. Performance-related concerns should be addressed as they arise. They should not be anticipated based on assumptions about age.

Key Points

- Productivity is rarely age-dependent. Employer attitude toward older workers is a major influence.
- The way managers treat older employees is critical to productivity, engagement, and morale.
- Boomers' informal role as key connectors is frequently overlooked.

- Because of their wisdom, experience, judgment, and soft-skill mastery, the productivity of mature workers often exceeds that of younger employees.

The Myth of Generational Performance Characteristics

In every arena there are some commonly held beliefs. The same is true of the workplace, where everyone knows we can expect people to perform according to the norms of their generational cohort. In short, generational stereotypes are excellent indicators of performance. After all, stereotypes are based on realities, which is why they're actually true – right?

We've all heard examples. "She's a millennial. You shouldn't expect loyalty." Or, "He's a boomer. He's earned the right to coast." And while we know that stereotyping people is a *bad* thing, we do it anyway. Psychologists call it confirmation bias. We categorize or pigeon-hole people as a way of reinforcing our beliefs – a kind of short cut to forming an opinion so we don't have to examine our attitudes more closely. It's reassuring to let ourselves off the hook by not requiring ourselves to be more rigorous in questioning our own beliefs or thinking more deeply at all (Nickerson 1998). Of course, some people label others because they foolishly believe that stereotypes are reliable predictors of behavior.

Stereotyping to account for personality traits is not an activity limited to North America. A recent study exploring the accuracy of stereotypes found that "Raters across nations tended to share similar beliefs about different age groups" (Chan et al. 2012). And regardless of whether we know better, in business every day, managers make decisions about performance based on generational stereotypes. Media outlets report daily on the behaviors and attitudes of one generation compared to the behaviors and attitudes of another, as if being part of a particular age-based cohort is the single prevailing factor for how one approaches work and life. Millennials are often cast as slackers or needy. Boomers, especially older boomers, are described as checked out, disengaged, or coasting. Poor performance and poor engagement remain unchecked or unaddressed or simply ignored as organizations fall victim to the belief that generational stereotypes are predictive of each employee's workplace behavior. Wouldn't it be futile to challenge a behavior that can't be changed? Of course it would!

The Reality

Our multicultural workplaces provide an interesting frame to help us understand that age-based stereotypes can be seriously damaging. In our global workplaces, we encounter employees with varying language fluency, employees who deal with time, urgency, and deadlines differently, and employees who have been exposed to technology to varying degrees – sometimes intensively and sometimes in limited ways. We meet with individuals with vastly different experiences and a variety of approaches to leadership and authority. We work with employees of diverse views and backgrounds, recognizing the value of their previous cultural experiences and integrating the best they bring into the existing culture of our own organization. At the same time, we expect all employees to perform, to meet expectations, and to adapt to our corporate norms. We are in complete agreement that cultural differences don't license poor performance, nor do they excuse managers from high expectations.

Recently, Lebo interviewed a European labor judge who has adjudicated hundreds of age-based discrimination cases. In the interview, the judge shone an interesting light on the subject of retirement. In her opinion, a mandated retirement age removes the obligation for an organization to discuss an employee's slipping performance or failure to measure up with an underachieving employee. In the opinion of this judge, mandated retirement is a shrewd mechanism created out of empathy with younger managers, a device that ignores the needs of older workers and allows their younger managers to avoid difficult conversations.

Our experience tells us that even if that is true, and even if generalizations are usually unwise, there are certain life experiences that shape the way different generations order and understand the world around them. And because common experiences create bonds, language, and predictable responses, some common characteristics can, in fact, sometimes be observed in any generational cohort. That's a reality – a reality that gives life to the foolish stereotype that paints everyone within a certain group with the same brush, no matter the evidence to the contrary.

Inclusion approaches can supercharge your generationally diverse workforce.

It's also a reality that North American organizations have long benefited from diverse groups of employees working within their walls. Indeed, Canada is a leader in multicultural workforces integrating the norms, cultures, and expectations of team mates from countries around the globe into cohesive teams that see value from this rich diversity (Klassen 2014). When new employees join organizations, managers work to integrate the value of what this new person brings to the team with the values that define the organizations' corporate culture.

Whether a new employee is from a different and distant country or merely a different sector, there is an understanding that a period of learning and integration is required for the employee to settle into a new role, team, and corporate culture. There is an expectation that company norms, expectations, and values will come to dictate the work that is to be done, and that performance and engagement will be measured against corporate standards. In other words, when you're invited to join the choir, you know there is an expectation that everyone sings from the same song book.

However, when it comes to age-based stereotypes, many organizations abandon the belief that corporate culture is the great unifier.

Whether the aging workforce is seen as a problem or as a competitive advantage depends on your corporate culture.

Generation-specific programs materialize in apparent sensitivity to particular cohorts, but in reality these programs normalize insensitivity and reinforce stereotypes that keep the employee experience divided. As a result, uncertainty and resentment are fostered between the generations. Older workers report feeling as if they are being ignored or pushed into "special projects" that lack purpose or real business value while training dollars are allocated to millennials. A pall that sometimes gathers around older workers, who begin to wonder if anyone values their contribution or cares about what they have to offer – what they *could* offer if only … They may even avoid contributing for fear of drawing attention to themselves and the differences they represent. As a result, their wisdom, enthusiasm, and creativity are lost.

Treating new graduates as special simply because they are young is as damaging a strategy as assuming boomers want to coast because they've been working a long time. Generation-based assumptions lead organizations to count out boomers decades before they are ready to leave the workforce. Generation-based assumptions are equally unfair to new workers, who are set up for a shock when they transition out of their employment honeymoon period into the real world of day-to-day work. Generation-based assumptions create conflict within the workforce and fail to maximize employee performance and satisfaction – with a direct effect on bottom-line results.

One example of generation-based programs and strategies is the current focus on knowledge transfer. Typically, knowledge-transfer programs match long-serving boomer employees with millennial new hires, the express goal being to transfer knowledge from one employee to another (Graham et al. 2006). Knowledge transfer implies that one employee has knowledge that needs to shift to another. But once shifted, the original employee's value or usefulness is diminished and the recipient's value is enhanced. Over the last decade, the health-sciences sector has recognized that this binary approach to knowledge does not serve research-focused activities well. There is an acknowledgment that not everything known needs to be transferred, that the recipient may interpret the information in a different way than the original possessor of the information, or that the recipient may use different tools or have different needs. There is also recognition that the context and environment within which that knowledge is being applied is shifting. As a result of these acknowledgments, new models of "knowledge translation" have emerged. In knowledge translation, both parties have an active role to identify, interpret, and convey what they know in a way that is meaningful and useful. Also, in assisting with translation, the original employee is not diminished. And, since knowledge does not necessarily need to be transferred from older workers to younger workers, using knowledge translation as a strategy removes the impetus for myth-reinforcing, generation-based workplace programs. As traditional silos are broken apart by evolving technologies, all employees across all functions, departments, geographies, and ages need ways to translate their knowledge and experiences. Knowledge translation may be the key.

Focus on knowledge transfer may indicate that your organization is falling victim to generational cohort myths.

Today, there is a bias in the research, as well as in practice, that seems to suggest engagement programs are only for the "young" and maintenance, transition, or "bridge" programs are what companies need for the "old." Apparently we are to believe that when employees reach a certain age they will naturally disengage from work. In fact, within the outplacement industry, this expectation is captured by an insensitive and unfortunate acronym: RIP, or "retired in place." Ironically, we are then surprised or disappointed when older workers appear less engaged in their work than they'd been earlier in their careers.

> Today's organizations anticipate and accelerate career stagnation.

But perhaps there is a better explanation for why older workers seem less enthusiastic about their work than they previously were – or as their younger colleagues now are. Perhaps it has nothing to do with age and everything to do with growth and opportunities versus stagnation and boredom.

By the time employees are in their fifties it is likely they have worked for their company or within the same industry or function for decades. While the world of work is always changing, at some point it is common for people to feel they're getting stale doing more or less the same work they've always done. But continuing on the same path is the easy way out. Plus, no change means no risk. At this point, they've built great skills, a good network, and a strong reputation in their field. They're in a safe place, so they become complacent. And while they hope for an opportunity to do something new, mostly they expect that something new and exciting will happen after retirement.

We see these workers all the time and we hear their stories. The closer they get to the traditional age of retirement, the more they believe there are few if any risk-free options for change. They stop asking for training at about the same time as their company stops having meaningful career conversations with them. By the time they're in their fifties, they begin to anticipate retirement, even look forward to it – not because they don't want to work, but because they see it as their only way out of stagnation and boredom. Many look forward to it as a long-awaited opportunity to dig in and accomplish something meaningful. The tedium of everyday routines uninterrupted by challenge or opportunities for growth can become overwhelmingly dreary.

In the 2015 movie *The Intern*, Robert De Niro plays a man in his seventies who is seeking an internship at an online retail company. As part of the interview process, the twenty-something manager takes him through the standard questions. When he gets to the question, "Where do you see yourself in ten years?" there are awkward laughs and agreement between the characters that the question isn't relevant.

Except that it is relevant! Why shouldn't De Niro's character have ideas of what he'd like to see happen over the next ten years? More to the point, it's no more likely that a twenty-five-year-old will express a desire to be with the same company in ten years than it is for an older worker. Indeed, when people are free of numerical constraints and stereotypical expectations, they can do wonderful things. At sixty-four, Jeff Bewkes, CEO of Time Warner, reshaped communications by selling his company to AT&T for $85 billion. At eighty-five, Warren Buffet was still CEO at Berkshire Hathaway. Hillary Clinton made her run for the presidency at sixty-eight. At seventy, Elton John announced his "retirement" and set out on a three-year concert tour.

No one should be exempt from the expectation of strong performance and high engagement.

Companies either have cultures that align an employee's work values, and with that of the larger organization, or they don't. As was described in chapter 4 with the Broken Talent Escalator, fostering a different culture or set of norms for each step is at best a formula for a suboptimal talent system, at worst a recipe for disaster. It is a mistake to assume that generational stereotypes are reliable predictors of behavior, and it is a major miscalculation to build an organization that treats groups of employees differently based on such mistaken assumptions.

Just as engagement is not required of one generation only, neither is performance – yet poor performance is routinely accommodated or overlooked in the boomer cohort. This accommodation isn't a kindness – it is an insult! Willingness to accept poor performance from any group is tantamount to posting a sign declaring that inadequacy is the best these slackers can achieve.

When Taylor and her team begin working in a new organization it is always a shock to hear about employees of all ages, often in key formal or informal leadership roles, who are underperforming without penalty. Either these organizations lack performance-management frameworks or they have not provided frontline managers with the support they need to take necessary action when performance fails to meet expectations. Managing workforce issues is usually a component of a manager's job while they maintain primary focus on their operational responsibilities, and there is a great deal of anxiety about the possible legal consequences of addressing employee performance issues. When the employee in question is an older worker, there tends to be even less focus on performance-based discussions than there might be with a younger employee. If the mature underperformers had fewer years of service and smaller severance requirements, it is likely they would be let go. But when that option is deemed too expensive or considered a legal risk, managers believe their only alternative is to find other ways to cover the work, leaving the older worker to underperform, even as job expectations are not met.

Organizations often chalk up underperformance to lack of engagement. Managers may feel powerless to confront the idler, hoping the situation will fix itself or go away. Then, too, they may fear a charge of ageism if they address performance concerns with the underachiever head-on. Either way, no direct action is taken. But failure to confront is no way to optimize an aging workforce. For some employees, the solutions described below will kick-start reengagement, and boost productivity and innovation in the very group most consider a lost cause.

It's important to keep in mind that as with any generational group, some boomers may simply be doing a bad job. An organization's failure to address poor performance ought not to be blamed on a generation's shortcomings, but should be recognized for what it is: a failure to manage – one that can be devastating to business. Whether an employee is twenty-seven or sixty-seven, managers must take action when performance is subpar. When age is taken out of the equation, appropriate action and the way forward are almost always perfectly clear.

There is a difference between performance management and career management. We don't advocate that poor performers be permitted to remain in their roles for as long as they like simply because people are living and working longer. We encourage quite the opposite: afford older workers the same consideration and set the same standards as those set for any other worker. Older workers, like younger ones, should be in a position to manage their own careers, including making decisions to attend training or to restructure instead of retiring – that is, to change roles or accept opportunities for growth and development.

"Older workers who find their work meaningful and engaging, experience high levels of job satisfaction, have not yet reached their professional goals and feel capable of taking on more responsibilities, are likely to continue working" (Smyer and Pitt-Catsouphes 2007).This suggests that older workers may prefer the experience of growth and forward momentum (i.e., thriving at work) over just maintaining their careers or disengaging in preparation for retirement. This view was supported in an AARP study in which nearly 90 percent of the respondents aged forty-five to seventy-four indicated that they were still growing in their work (Hewitt 2015).

Eliminate the Age-Based Workplace

It is a mistake to define an organization's culture by generational segments. For the first time in the modern era, it is common for people of grandparent (or even great-grandparent) and grandchild age to be working side by side. We encourage employers to consider the generational characteristics that should be acknowledged with sensitivity and those that are simply a function of youth. Older workers are disengaged at work from time to time, yes, but no more than younger workers, who are sometimes disengaged too. The solution is not to assume that chronological age is the driver of disengagement. It is to examine personal career-development supports and organizational culture to identify the source of the issue.

Key Points

"Culture" means "the way we do things around here," and the goal of fixing the issue of disparate expectations is to use corporate culture as the big unifier. Rather than isolating specific demographic groups and expecting more of one group and less of another, or excusing certain behaviors that are counter to corporate culture and accepting them as simply a function of age, companies would be wise to use the same approaches and materials to support their intergenerational workforce as they do their multicultural workforce. Namely:

- Recognize that the workplace requires everyone to adapt to new cultural norms. ("We have a way of doing what we do around

here and we should all be singing from the same song book.")
New graduates must migrate from student culture to work
culture. Boomers are migrating from traditional career structures
to more freelance-based structures with Legacy Career options.
Consider how employees of all ages are adjusting to the new
world of work. Identify what tools you can leverage from your
multicultural workforce to help employees of all ages

- gain new language fluency, especially around technical
  ideas and tools;
- adjust to more collaborative work processes;
- and adjust to physical changes in the work environment,
  such as working from home, working remotely, or sharing
  work stations.

These examples all have cultural impacts. They are markers
indicating that things are not the same as they used to be. It is
not age that determines who performs well in the new environment but adaptability – the ability to adjust to new expectations
and changing norms. The first step is to be clear and explicit
when norms have changed.

- Clearly identify what you expect from your managers as they
  work with their staff. Are they incentivized to have good career
  conversations with all employees? Do they have the tools and
  the skills to address employees' questions and concerns? Do
  they know how to separate career discussions from performance
  discussions?
- Identify the source of skill-related deficiencies and evaluate
  training policies. Are you using sound learning practices to
  ensure ongoing skill development? As new technology emerges,
  how are you ensuring that all employees have access to read
  about, discuss, try, and evaluate new tools?
- Challenge cultural assumptions that work needs to be done as it
  always has been done while resisting the tendency to turn to
  younger employees for innovative practices. Spend time as a

leadership team defining what innovation-related competency looks like for new graduates, high performers (the experts), and high potentials (the future leaders). Consider using a maturity-matrix approach to set out expectations and convey a culture that values age-blind innovation.

- Ensure that gaps between your corporate culture's norms and expectations and individual performances are addressed.

8

FROM MYTH TO SMART STRATEGY

Over the last fifteen years, corporations have experimented with a variety of ways to make the best use of their workforces. Creative solutions have ranged from employing a workforce of full-time employees, to outsourcing noncore functions, to outsourcing core functions and retaining market-facing activities, to offshoring, insourcing, and leveraging contingent models. We've seen them all. At the core of each decision to change, shift, or abandon a particular labor strategy is a business goal based on the answer to the company's key business question: how can the organization do what it does better, faster, cheaper, and more effectively than the competition?

They've tried it all and nobody is happy. As in past generations, younger employees want to have management responsibilities more quickly than traditional paths allow. But a closer look reveals there is, in fact, something new happening: many older employees want to be engaged and working in roles that *don't* involve significant people-management responsibility – typically a hallmark of senior roles. Millennials want senior roles. Forgotten Generation X just wants to be recognized for their work while balancing ever-increasing home and work demands.

More valuable than ever are people who know how to get things done, who are well networked and who have expertise not easily found by a search engine. Yet the employees who best fit this description – the mature population – are routinely sidelined, rarely asked to be the internal source of wisdom they could be, stymied and stifled by stereotypes, assumptions, politics, structures, and a belief that they must leave an organization without ever having had their value actualized as an internal consultant.

J. Bersin, a research analyst and principal at Bersin by Deloitte, writes about talent management and the need for talent mobility: "In today's business environment this includes lateral movement, upward movement within a role, movement into leadership, movement into international assignments, movement into functional specialties, movement into developmental or exploratory assignments, and often movement from part-time to full-time or vice-versa" (Bersin 2010). If you recognize the unique skill sets of every individual within your workforce and the talent gaps you want to fill, the possibilities are infinite.

Older workers have the polished soft skills necessary for thriving in the new economy.

The Aging Workforce Will Migrate to Today's Working Environment (If They Haven't Already)

In *Digital Natives, Digital Immigrants* (2001), educator M. Prensky emphasized how important it is for educators to recognize a shift in the way new generations access and process information. He stressed the importance of understanding that the difference is not limited to the use of technology, but includes language, learning style, and the way individuals interact with each other. Prensky's idea was later expanded to embrace the concept of the digital visitor and the digital immigrant to explain different generations' relationships and facility with technology.

We wish to extend this concept from the world of technology to the general state of the workplace. If millennials are digital natives, we suggest they are also natives to the freelance economy and the rest of us are simply visitors or immigrants to this new arrangement.

It's often said that many of today's top jobs did not exist ten years ago, nor were they even imagined. We hear this statement and think of the young. We consider the implications of that statement to post-secondary education and what is now required to prepare students for their futures. We think of our children and grandchildren and

	MILLENNIAL	GEN X	BOOMER
DIGITAL (Technology)	Native	Fluent/ Slight Accent	Slight Accent/ Accent
FREELANCE ECONOMY	Native	Native/ Slight Accent	Visitor
EXISTING CORPORATE CULTURES	Visitor Newcomer	Native	Native

Comparing Generations as Natives or Immigrants to Key Workforce Trends

how quickly they learn to use devices or tools that take us hours or days to understand – if we ever really do. We see increased funding for tech start-ups and companies, realizing that, in the main, the founders will be between the ages of eighteen and thirty-five.

But it's a mistake to consider the freelance economy and new technologies as belonging more to one generation than another. The freelance economy describes the basic underlying market conditions in which all generations are now working. The workers are the building blocks of today's workplaces, with surprising pockets of hidden talent and expertise that are completely missed or overlooked when age-based assumptions are accepted as truth.

Millennials did not create today's workplace conditions. They graduated into them.

Example: Social Media Use #1

Increasingly, employees in a high-tech firm were found to be using social media tools to communicate with each other and with clients. One recent graduate working as a customer service representative had been exchanging messages with a customer over the course of the day in an attempt to resolve a customer service issue. At the end of the day, the supervisor reviewed the logs of the interactions and found that the tone of the employee's messages had caused misunderstandings about the status of an order – specifically, about when delivery could be expected and what information was required. The employee had included these details in his messages but his casual tone had not instilled confidence. Nor did it reflect an understanding of the customer's urgency.

When the supervisor spoke with the employee, he could see that the employee fully understood the importance of the order and had taken all the right steps to ensure it was expedited. What's more, the employee had provided updates all along the way to keep the customer informed. Indeed, he had sent so many updates in short bits and pieces that the overall message and its meaning had been lost along the way. Despite being in full control and attending directly to the customer's needs, the employee had represented the company as scattered and unreliable. The employee's facility and familiarity with the technology had not helped him convey the customer-centric service message his company valued. Indeed, it achieved quite the opposite.

Example: Social Media Use #2

An intern at a chemical-processing company was looking for information about an upcoming product launch. He'd been told he was going to be working on this project and wanted to be prepared. Since his manager was not available, when the intern ran into the president in the hallway, he asked if the president could help him get the product launch plans that afternoon. The president said the information the intern wanted was kept at head office in Europe, and suggested he speak with his manager to request the relevant information.

But the intern wanted to do a good job and didn't want to delay getting started until his manager returned. He thought it wiser to gather the required information and take it to his manager when they met later in the week. He was certain that at that point he could get guidance on next steps.

The intern found the firm's global CEO in the company directory and emailed his request, but the CEO had decided only the previous day not to proceed with the product. The request for information triggered a series of escalations and concerns about leaks, confidentiality, and a lack of control in the Canadian operations.

Both case studies come from Taylor's real client examples that demonstrate that knowing how to use a technology and using it well are two different things. In both cases, the assumption that information can and should flow freely led to serious misunderstandings. In the second example, the eager intern was fired.

We showcase these case studies as examples of how being comfortable or even nimble using social media tools is not enough to do the job well. And if you compare teaching someone how to use a messaging app with which they are unfamiliar and teaching someone good communication skills, it's instantly clear that teaching the tools of the technology is the easy part. And keep in mind that while older workers are often assumed to have weaker technology skills than their younger colleagues, 64 percent of people over fifty use Facebook and nearly half of people sixty-five and older use it too (Duggan 2015).

Interestingly, younger employees were the very cohort routinely sent to Lebo's communication workshops in the Fortune 500 companies for which she worked. Aware of skill gaps in their younger team members, managers were eager to help them build the skills they needed in a competitive marketplace. But these programs have decreased in frequency with tightened budgets and other urgencies. What's more, smaller companies and start-ups often have more pressing priorities, or may not even be aware there is a gap between technological savvy and communication competency.

It's true that many older workers need training and exposure to the tools of today's technology to gain confidence and competence in using them, just as any other worker might need. However, what older workers may have by default is the judgment, experience, and perhaps even the training, to know how best to use the tools to achieve the specific goal. Older workers may have learned long ago – by experience or education – how to massage a message, when to ensure a direct conversation, the ideal frequency for updates, how to take care with an e-mail to be sure it is not misunderstood, how best to address concerns to deescalate issues and handle the customer so everybody wins. The technology is just the tool; the purpose of these tools is to sell, build relationships, expand context, make connections, or expedite service – and these are things experienced workers know how to do.

Likewise, youth are often seen as being more entrepreneurial or comfortable with the ebbs and flows of today's working arrangements than their older coworkers. They are perceived as seeking more flexibility and being readier for change. Indeed, they have graduated into an environment where instability and flexibility are to be expected; it is their native world. But that doesn't mean that they are better suited to succeed in chaotic conditions than their older colleagues. It is a mistake to confuse comfort with competence. Younger employees facing career uncertainty may have peers in similar circumstances, but they lack a knapsack of experiences and tools to help them navigate and succeed. Older employees may experience distress by the shifting nature of their relationships with their employers, and they may feel unsettled and at risk, but they have lots of skills to help them find their way.

Part Three

CAPITALIZING ON THE INTERGENERATIONAL WORKFORCE

9

GETTING FOCUSED: TOOLS AND APPROACHES

We began by zooming out to examine the macro trends governing the future of work, work-related revolutions, and aging. Next, we narrowed our lens to examine talent structures, especially talent escalators. We confronted common myths that prevent essential change and keep talent stuck on inefficient talent escalators. With this understanding of the impact that outdated career thinking can have on the employees within your organization, we now zoom in to reveal how you can ensure your organization is ready for the talent revolution.

Different Actions for Different Actors

In 2017, Taylor consulted with more than 100 organizations and presented at 30 conferences to a total audience of more than 3,000 leaders. Some of the people with whom she spoke were C-level executives. Others were managers within organizations. Still others were on the front line of a changing employment landscape. These included social workers, career counselors, and career practitioners. Time after time, discussions about longevity and changes in the workforce would bounce from broad, sweeping trends and policy implications to very personal, individual discussions. Often, after meeting with a senior executive team about an organization's approach to succession planning and intergenerational strategies, one of the senior leaders would call Taylor, eager to share their personal uncertainty or apprehension about what might be next in their own career. It was a constant reminder that the talent revolution is at once a strategic and a deeply personal experience for everyone currently in the workforce.

There are three distinct categories of actors in the talent revolution for whom we have written this book: CEOs, HR leaders, and frontline managers. In each of these roles, there are organizational, team, and individual responsibilities with connections to a changing career time line. We've taken a time-horizon approach to identifying the different actions and concerns on which each role should focus (Jaques 2017). This takes into account that individuals have different levels of proficiency when it comes to anticipating, integrating, and understanding the future. According to the time-horizon theory, all employees within an organization have the capacity to operate within time frames of three months to twenty years (The Economist 2009). Successful C-level executives can work with twenty-year time horizons, whereas frontline staff generally operate within three- or six-month time frames. When people are promoted beyond their time-horizon capacity, the organization suffers.

The talent revolution requires action within different time frames. CEOs must be visionaries looking beyond 2030, understanding how demographics and longevity will impact long-term strategy, markets, and industry structures. Indeed, CEOs need to understand that this one driver accelerates and supports the other four future of work drivers. At the same time, HR leaders need to focus on what will happen between now and 2030 as their organizations navigate workplace shifts prompted by boomers who are redefining careers and working life. It is HR's responsibility to concentrate on culture- and workforce-based competitive advantages. Simultaneously, frontline managers need tools for helping their staff understand and adapt to a world of work that is changing quickly – recognizing that personal, departmental, and operational impacts are likely within the next twelve to sixty months.

The next three chapters provide additional insight, resources, and recommendations for each of the three main actors in the talent revolution. Chapter 10 focuses on the long-term structural questions we hear from CEOs. Chapter 11 outlines key strategic frameworks and actions for today's CHROs to consider. Chapter 12 identifies specific actions and needs for frontline managers as they bridge corporate strategy and everyday employee experience, conducting career conversations, performance-management discussions, and workforce-planning activities.

Key Points

- CEOs must think long-term and deduce how demographics will impact long-term strategy, markets, and industry structures.
- HR leaders must focus on the next few years and concentrate on culture- and workforce-based competitive advantage.
- Frontline managers must think one to five years out and develop skills to help staff understand and adapt to a changing workplace.

10

CRITICAL ACTIONS FOR CEOS

Longevity as a Competitive Advantage

Today's CEOs work in an environment that demands annual if not quarterly results, even as technology-powered industry shifts occur. Leaders must be able to balance short-term performance requirements with strategies that anticipate new structures, players, and competitors – elements that may not become clear for several more years. It is a tricky business managing the moment and envisioning a future state almost impossible to picture, but in the last decade, the need for CEOs to predict, place bets, and pivot quickly has been written about frequently, often with a focus on product mix, financing structures, globalization strategies, and partnership possibilities. Now in the talent revolution, we see an ever-increasing flow of workforce-related issues making it to the CEO's and board's agendas as they grapple with concerns like succession planning and leadership development. Motivated by the reality that by 2030 a large percentage of the existing workforce will have exited, many CEOs and organizations are seeking new sources of talent to backfill gaps, receive transferred knowledge, and propel existing cultures and business models into new ways of working. Century-old insurance companies want to reinvent themselves as nimble technology firms. Professional services firms are challenging the idea that "manager" is a promotion, moving instead to position it as a frontline role in which the employee happens to have significant people-management skills rather than merely a gift for mastering spreadsheets or creating presentations. As the "old guard" moves out of the organization there is a sense that whatever comes next will be more than a replacement. It will be substantively different.

But if we've learned anything in our research for this book and our work with organizations over the last five years, it is that by 2030 more seventy- and eighty-year-olds will continue to be engaged in work than ever before. Whether it is in part-time, full-time, advisory, volunteer, or other roles, today's boomers will capitalize on the bonus years their longevity has given them and establish new ways in which work and life can be interwoven as part of their Legacy Career phase of life.

Smart CEOs will shift their thinking about succession planning. It is now important to contemplate workforce structures that focus less on short-term knowledge transfer and more on cultivating lifelong, sustainable, affordable, and profitable relationships that foster ongoing knowledge translation and engagement. CEOs need to consider how to value and profit from employee relationships over time.

A quick Google search of "employees are our greatest asset" returns more than 21 million hits. One of the results is a meme that states:

"'Our employees are our greatest asset' – source: every CEO everywhere."

We know that employers mean well when they say their employees are assets. We understand they want to convey the prioritization of people over property. We realize they want to telegraph their respect and value for the people who work in their organization. But over the last decade, while the employer-employee relationship has changed in a dozen different ways, management's rhetoric about the importance of their employees to the success of the business has become so commonplace it has lost almost all meaning. The words rarely reflect action, and to an employee, it is a lot like hearing, "Your call is important to us" as you wait on hold for an hour. Do you believe it?

Good intentions aside, consider what accountants define as an asset – and it isn't people. Assets are acquired at a value, depreciate over time as they are used up, and then are written off and labeled "fully depreciated" at the end of their usefulness. Calling people your greatest assets is not only a linguistic mistake, it is a strategic one too, because it informs the way you make decisions. If, as an employer, you want to use accounting terms to describe your relationship with your employees, we suggest you consider your workforce as talent equity.

 Employees are not assets.

Of course, it's easier for employees to think of themselves as assets as they're being shuffled around than it is to consider themselves equity, which implies responsibility for continuously increasing value – personal as well as corporate. But equity is the way to go. Here's why.

We ask you to think of *equity* as the value of *something* to its owners – in this case, the value of talent to the company employing that talent. We use talent equity as a metric in the talent revolution to measure the workforce's value to the business. While assets are continuously depreciating until any value has vanished, equity grows. An equity approach looks at today's investment in terms of the future value. Our hope is that HR and managers will become talent-equity leaders, not people-as-assets managers.

Why the Asset vs. Equity Distinction Matters

The distinction matters because it's more than mere semantics. In chapter 2 we described how revolutions are messy and why it takes time for the debris to settle and the way forward to be clear. Since the revolution we are currently experiencing is still in its early stages, we can't possibly guess what lies ahead. What we do know for certain is that our current asset-focused thinking will keep us mired in the past, and that we need a different framework to promote thinking in new and different ways. An equity framework works because it's long-term and more about abundance than scarcity. Furthermore, when you think of employees as equity, keeping in mind that equity grows with time, it upends the way you value the older members of your workforce. As we've discussed, there is an abundance of talent that creative organizations can access from within and from without, none of which looks anything like your current workforce structure. Now we're talking about *doing more with more* – while increasing the value to both the company and the employee.

Talent equity is about doing more with more.

And that's not all. An equity perspective makes it easier to make decisions about how to replace or restructure a Broken Talent Escalator. Right now, your escalator manages one step at a time and attempts to optimize what happens on each step – but it's the whole structure that's the problem. You can optimize all you want on one step or another and never achieve the potential value embodied in the people on the other steps. The total structure is a teardown.

New Thinking about Talent as Equity

In accountancy these days, there are calls for new ways to express value within a company. In their book *The End of Accounting and the Path Forward for Investors*, Professors Baruch Lev and Feng Gu, of NYU's Stern School of Business and the University of Buffalo, respectively, remind laypeople that financial reports focus on historical values (Lev and Gu 2016). That is, they explain what has already happened and because they do, they are ill-suited to looking ahead. Lev reports that the accounting industry has undergone many revolutions in its over six-hundred-year history, and he believes it is in the midst of the next wave of change tied to a revolution in company business models (Vogel 2016). He notes that today, value in an organization is tied to patents, technology, and other intangibles that contribute to an organization's innovation, but that financial reporting practices do not recognize the human shift that has taken place concurrently. Says Lev: "Value is no longer created by physical assets; they are at best enablers. Value is created by innovation. But accounting is stuck in the Industrial Age" (quoted in Vogel 2016, 36).

Lev uses the acquisition of research to prove his point, arguing that there is no economic difference between purchasing research from another organization and paying in-house researchers to do the work. But in their financial statements, companies that acquire research *appear* more profitable than those that hire their own researchers because there is no place to capture the future value of the experience and expertise acquired in the in-house development of the research. It is an intangible, the potential value of which has no place in financial reporting. Indeed, many company expenses today are, in effect, investments with future benefits. Lev insists that traditional balance sheets fail to reflect those assets in a way that is useful, and he calls for more recognition that today's investments are made in intangible assets. Of course, assets don't appear on the income statement; they appear on the balance sheet, and intangible assets have to pass the test of satisfying a long-term benefit.

All this brings us back to what it means for CEOs to declare employees their company's greatest assets – an unapologetic reminder that people are written off long before their full value has been realized in an environment where on a daily basis both employer and employee demonstrate only short-term thinking.

Balance-Sheet Thinking

Financial considerations tend to dominate corporate strategy and boardroom discussions, and as everyone searches for cost-cutting opportunities, it's hard to counter arguments for strategies rooted in a company's financial well-being. After all, companies are generally judged by the health of their financial statements and reports. But when it comes to the workforce, reports can be misleading or even wrong because an employee's value extends well beyond the years they are employed by the company. Yet balance sheets fail to take the long-term value of the employer-employee relationship into account. Still, smart companies, like technology providers Conenza and Enterprise Jungle, are highlighting, calculating, and supercharging the intangible value of their organization's alumni network. They know – as you should too – that employees convey your brand and represent value to you even when they no longer collect a paycheck from you.

Without new thinking and a shift in tone, executive teams will continue to treat employees as assets to be used and discarded, all the while professing to value them. True value lies in an equity mindset, where the employee's long-term desire to remain engaged increases and profits rise to the benefit of all stakeholders.

Recommendations for CEOs

Shifting from an asset to an equity mindset vis-à-vis talent requires a long-term, strategic view of the workforce – even as the average length of employment continues to plummet. It may seem counterintuitive, but as the speed at which employees leave accelerates, either because of retirements or other reasons, CEOs need to implement strategic frameworks and policies that help leadership teams thrive while working with constantly shifting talent pools. They must also rethink their relationship with their HR leaders and inspire them to step out from behind operational mandates to become the revolutionary leaders required to ensure that organizations capitalize on workforce trends and reap competitive advantages rather than merely reacting from behind the curve. Indeed, CEOs need to raise the expectations to which they hold CHROs while rejecting the commonly held age-related myths and ensuring that ageism does not limit the organization's ability to reap the benefits of talent equity across the workforce's entire working life.

Supercharge Your Workforce with CHROs as Managers of Talent Equity

In the Technological Revolution we saw VPs of IT emerge from being the head of a critical function area to become chief information officers (or CIOs) – strategic leaders working hand in hand with the CEO and CFO to ensure that long-term strategic investments enhanced corporate competitiveness – with the right infrastructure to support the organization's strategic plan. Today, HR representatives are valued members of the senior leadership team and critical members of business-partner relationships across the organization. But many have not yet stepped into the evolving and necessary strategic role they must play to lead organizations through a revolution that is all about talent. This is a new and essential role for HR representatives, and they must master it.

Brands have value in the marketplace (Keller 2003). Value is equity. Equity grows over time, and if leaders want a good financial-statement anchor for an approach to talent that conveys the importance and value of the workforce, a focus on equity is the way to go. Consider the difference in role description and expectations if someone is a manager of assets, with the inevitable focus on efficiency, compared to the priorities of someone who manages equity, focusing on the future realization of value from today's investments. HR leaders have long acted as asset managers, concentrating on the health of the current workforce. In that role, workforce-related programs and expenditures are costs and any workforce program that has a future financial obligation becomes a liability. The value of knowledge gained by employees is not calculated. That is, employees are valued the same last year as they will be this year without any way to account for improvements or developments essential for creativity and innovation – this at precisely the time that innovation is the most expensive commodity of all.

If there is no appreciation that employees increase in value over time, we are back to Lev's accounting-based dilemma that financial statements do not accurately account for innovation. In the case of a workforce, the "employees-as-asset" approach results in strategies and programs that, given today's employee longevity, rely on unrealistically short career paths, a lack of recognition for the equity value in the alumni population, and a short-term focus on fighting today's workforce emergency rather than using longer-term workforce demographics to reduce the often whiplash-inducing approach to radical swings in policies and priorities.

Talent equity shifts the thinking from managing individual employees and overall expense lines to focusing on longer-term investments that deliver specific business value. Long-term thinking gives rise to revamped, updated approaches to career-path structures and employee relationships, which we will address in the next chapter. Equity-based job descriptions anticipate a shared responsibility for an employee to know more, to be better, and to increase their positive impact every year. It stimulates self-actualization. It supercharges organizations by concentrating on increasing value-demanding programs, policies, and changes that encourage the creation of value and that eliminate complacency and coasting. It is the CEO's role to ensure they have the CHRO partner they need for the revolutionary change that will propel the organization forward.

Observations from the Field

In 2014, Company Q faced a critical succession problem given that over 55 percent of their workforce was past the age of pension eligibility. They called on Taylor to address their demographic and intergenerational challenges with a specific request to create a program for new apprentices. These apprentices would be hired from postsecondary programs and developed into leaders who could fill the gaps left by retiring employees. The company believed it needed more than a thousand new hires every year for the next five years, but the recruitment folks were tapped out, understaffed, and unable to keep up with all of the business requests they received.

Once engaged, Taylor's team developed a workforce model based on assumptions about attrition, retirement, and alumni engagement that predicted how the workforce would change over the next ten years. When coupled with market data, it became obvious that the leadership gap would reach a crisis within eighteen months – a disastrously short time period, since apprentices needed twenty-four months to prepare for entry-level, non-leadership roles. Investing in rapid onboarding and leadership-acceleration programs might help a little, but would not resolve the impending crisis.

Despite past reliance on graduate hiring to replenish workforce assets (employees), the frenzied on-campus hiring to fill gaps left by retiring staff was a poor use of recruiter time and effort. This company needed to shift from a strictly "grow from within" organization to one with a 5–8 year focus on recruiting hires with 5–10 years of experience so they could hit the road running. Plus, the company needed to accept the fact that leaders could come from outside and be respected and valued. Shortsightedness had created a calamity.

Supercharge Your Workforce with Age-Aware CEOs

In a study on age discrimination and paid work in Canada, researchers E.D. Berger and D. Hodgins contend that workplace ageism persists, and that in addition to forcing older workers to retire, it "directly impacts older worker retention, training, and recruitment" (Berger and Hodgins 2012, 1). Ageist language, policies, comments, and even jokes serve only to keep your organization stuck in a neutral zone and make it clear that you are not revolution-ready, that you are not invested in your employees as equity, and that you do not see a future for the older workers currently within your ranks or for those who will soon join them.

Ageism is hard to combat, often because it is hard to recognize. While there are still many examples of sexism, racism, and homophobia in organizations, when a sexist comment is made, everyone knows it – and this usually includes the person making the comment. But people make ageist comments all the time completely oblivious to the underlying meaning or implications of their words. What's more, we know that older workers themselves often fail to recognize that their own language and attitude towards aging is ageist. We call this "casual ageism," an attitude so deeply entrenched in the culture that it would be folly to insist there is an explicit intention to harm. Moreover, often the very people involved in an ageist exchange would categorically reject it as ageist.

In part 2 we outlined five common myths that drive ageist behaviors and policies in the workplace. While most of today's technological innovation was born of boomer brains and implemented by intergenerational teams of boomers, millennials, and Gen Xers, today those very same boomers are being marginalized. CEOs must ensure they have their own company-specific data that gets beyond stereotypes and anecdotes about older workers. At the same time, they must help shift organizational culture into an inclusive one. They need to remind their leadership teams to manage poor performance in any cohort through specific interventions and not to attribute deficiencies to age – either as a tactic for excusing poor performance or to justify the withholding of access to new training, thinking, and tools.

How often do we hear of a founding CEO who comes into the office every day, well into their eighties, not merely to maintain connections with colleagues and the company they love, but to contribute in ways that are significant for the future of the organization? Cultural norms and expectations are powerful influencers. Entrepreneurial spirit and lifelong learning is killed not by age but by corporate culture. In the talent revolution, CEOs must reveal possibilities, model desirable behaviors, and create healthy workplaces for themselves and their employees, regardless of age.

Action Steps for CEOs

Cultural Level

These are actions that require changes in the way your organization thinks and acts related to working-life expectancy, productivity, and intergenerational expectations.

- Update organizational thinking and mindset about careers and longevity (discussed in chapters 1 and 3).
- Individualize talent management and career-path programs; avoid "generation-based" assumptions as a foundation for employee grouping (discussed in chapter 7).

Strategic Level

These are actions that require changes in workforce structures, focus, metrics, and measurable behaviors.

- Outline ten-year flexible roadmap to ensure the right balance between managing chronic conditions and dealing with acute or urgent issues appropriately – and knowing which is which (discussed in chapter 1).
- Identify supporting structures, skills, metrics, and resources needed with ongoing feedback and measurement (discussed in chapter 4).
- Lead organization in pivots and shifts to optimize market position and return on employee engagement (discussed in chapter 2).

Operational Level

These are actions that present you with new information, choices, and approaches to attract, manage, motivate, and retain workers of all ages.

- Focus on the shorter term; rely on data and direction to navigate over the next few months and years.
- Concentrate on implementation, consistency, maintaining focus, and providing optimal conditions, resources, and supports.
- Support deep career-management competency and awareness.
- Require frontline roles to identify gaps and issues in culture and strategy; recognize these as symptoms and develop the skills for addressing them.

Key Points

- Workforce longevity is a competitive advantage.
- Consider employees talent equity rather than assets, and do more with more.
- HR needs to step forward and take a strategic role.
- CEOs must create an age-inclusive culture to reap the benefits of longevity and realize a competitive advantage.

11

CRITICAL ACTIONS
FOR HR LEADERS

In chapter 10 we discussed the importance of elevating the role of HR leaders. Currently members of the executive team, they must become the revolutionary CHRO leaders organizations need to capitalize on the workforce opportunities provided by added decades of productivity. Today's HR leaders share the responsibility of stepping into these elevated roles by recognizing that their responsibilities have expanded, and are more important than ever. Now is the time for the CHRO to focus on culture – especially in today's era of a flexible, transient, and evolving workforce. Further, it is time to

identify new workforce and career-management structures and relationships, recognizing the value of the Legacy Career phase of life
with new career models and alumni programs. Finally, CHROs need
to help frontline managers normalize more frequent comings and
goings from their teams, developing different skills related to career
management, succession planning, and knowledge translation.

Supercharge Your Workforce with Culture Models for Revolutionary Times

William Bridges's seminal work on change management identifies
three specific states through which individuals and organizations
must pass when dealing with change (Bridges and Mitchell 2000).
The model highlights the emotional stages associated with any
change process: endings, the neutral zone, and new beginnings.
Using Bridges's model to discuss the way changes in today's
workplaces are experienced by the mature workforce, we can better understand how organizations can help employees as they
find their way through the neutral zone and successfully shift to
the new world of work, where many long-standing beliefs are
challenged.

Right now, we are in the early days of a neutral zone. Technology
has ushered in an era in which so much flexibility is possible that
many of the core tenants and assumptions about work no longer
hold true. Machines do work that used to require human labor – and
lots of it. We can partner and collaborate with colleagues across time
zones and even languages with ease and at minimal or no financial
cost. Our devices provide us with access to information that past
generations would have needed decades to acquire. Empires are
started in garages and at dining room tables, and today, the largest
companies in almost any sector don't actually own any of the goods
they sell. Indeed, "Uber, the world's largest taxi company, owns no

vehicles. Facebook, the world's most popular media owner, creates no content. Alibaba, the most valuable retailer, has no inventory. And Airbnb, the world's largest accommodation provider, owns no real estate. Something interesting is happening" (Goodwin 2015).

But these changes, with all the promise they hold for a very different future, also serve as a warning that the way organizations and employees once related to each other has dramatically changed – and that change, especially for many older workers, marks the end of an era.

It is important to acknowledge endings. In our revolutionary phases, endings come just before the next revolutionary cycle and the chaotic, confusing, and contradictory period where workplace whiplash is likely to occur when new ideas are tested without a clear pathway to the future. The period after an ending has all of the characteristics of the neutral zone. While some individuals may still be mourning the past, others may be in a state of turmoil, struggling to see what will come next and finding few answers.

We are currently in a neutral zone vis-à-vis career models and, especially, career models for the over 58.8 million Americans between the ages of fifty and sixty-four (Baker et al. 2014). Never before have we considered our reasonable work-life expectations to extend into our sixties, seventies, and even our eighties, and there is no doubt that we are in uncharted territory. It feels like the calm before the storm – static and leaden. But with new horizons come new opportunities. The task of business leaders is to create and share a vision with those who are struggling to free themselves from the shackles of the past and help them move from what was to what can be.

Strong cultures are built on strong relationships, and in their work Dave Logan, John King, and Halee Fischer-Wright (2008) identify the strength and power of triadic relationships. Groups of three are both a self-reinforcing structure and a natural way for people to engage with each other. To turn an aging workforce into a competitive advantage, three corporate functions must be aligned and made to work together. Only then will the key ideas and action items take hold.

Today's VPs and senior VPs of HR need to step up to become tomorrow's CHROs, and to ensure that the long-term equity of the workforce is maximized with the right talent infrastructure to support the strategy.

Tomorrow's CHROs need to lead executive teams through the changing nature of the world of work. They must determine the way talent platforms and structures will transform who does what within the organization. In the case of the aging workforce, CHROs must start with the leadership team to demonstrate how intergenerational approaches that span the full working-life continuum can lead to greater workforce collaboration, efficiency, and innovation. Like their IT colleagues in the mid- to late 1990s who moved from being VPs of IT to the elevated position of CIO, HR leaders cannot make this transition into a CHRO role alone. Others around the executive table must recognize that the critical competence, skill, and analysis required to make sense of the changing workforce resides in the senior HR leader – and that confidence must be earned. Luckily, HR has the support of the other members of the talent revolution triad, and can rely on partners with analytics and communications expertise.

To be leaders of the talent revolution, HR managers must claim their due and rely on sound, relevant, and granular data. Too often HR is faced with a mandate to solve the succession concerns of an aging workforce. They know the average age of their workforce – perhaps even down to the departmental level – and they begin to recommend programs and approaches to lower the age. The average age of your workforce is a good example of a meaningless metric that feels like it should be important but is not. The overall average age is as useless in helping leaders identify where there is trapped talent equity potential (described in chapter 10) as it is in divining which teams within your organization are at greatest risk as demographic shifts occur. It's equally ineffective at revealing which departments are most suited to Legacy Career paths that might draw employees from across the organization. Nor will knowing the average age of your workforce illuminate how the organization might be best served by creating or leveraging talent platform strategies that capitalize on the freelance economy in ways that include existing talent.

Many HR leaders recognize and rely on the expertise of data analysts as integral members of their teams (Bersin 2012). But just as there is an evolution from VP HR to CHRO, so, too, must workforce data analysts build new, future-focused models that provide the data required – which is often very different from what is usually requested by leaders not trained in analytics. Once the data are available, HR can look to its partner in employee communications for guidance on how best to share the information with their executive colleagues, leadership teams, and employees.

While HR and employee communications are typically aligned on organizational charts, they don't routinely rely on each other as critical triad partners. In these changing times, the way messages are conveyed is more critical than ever before. Since any change that affects the workforce has the potential to be stressful, and every change will certainly feel intensely personal, getting the messaging, timing, reinforcement, and support exactly right is critical.

Right now, up and down your Broken Talent Escalator, there are vigorous discussions among employees, managers, freelancers, and candidates as they try to determine the extent of your commitment to the success of their careers. While noble aphorisms and lofty speeches may fuel these discussions, your actions are evidence of the values you hold, and as we all know, actions speak louder than words. Consider these examples of corporate messaging distressingly tone deaf to the employee experience.

"Respect" is a component of many organizations' corporate values, yet leaders behave as if the word doesn't exist. Consider companies in the process of reorganization. Commonly, just minutes after the announcement is made, selected employees are walked out the door for fear of security breaches. Before their walk of shame, these same employees are carefully watched while they pack up their things and IT terminates their access to files, phone, and digital equipment. The whole process is humiliating and painful on many levels – and nobody sees it more clearly than the workers who remain. There is little anyone can say in the way of platitudes or speeches to counteract the clear disrespect for employees that these actions broadcast.

And what about companies that require everyone in the trenches to tighten their belts and cut costs while leaders flout outlandish expenditures? Isn't that a clear statement of privilege versus underclass? Why pretend "our employees are our greatest assets" when executive-level behaviors make it perfectly clear that leadership thinks something else entirely?

The importance of aligning corporate values with corporate communications cannot be overstated. Similarly, aligning leadership behaviors with the corporate *pitch* is essential too. It's best to start with the truth, and to assert that your employees are your greatest assets is not only gratuitous and self-serving – it doesn't *feel* true to the very people you're talking about. Plus, it overlooks the critical and mutually respectful relationship that high-performing companies have with their workforces – where focus is on the creation and growth of value both for the organization and for the individual. In short, as we discussed in chapter 10, the asset-focused employer-employee relationship is unwise. If senior leadership teams and HR leaders rely on outdated platitudes, they are missing out on an opportunity to capitalize on changing workforce dynamics. It is not in leadership's interest to perpetuate the sentiment that employees are assets – valued or otherwise. Leaders must rethink their pitch and consider their workforce as talent equity, not assets.

Profit from Alumni Talent Equity by Normalizing Legacy Careers

Retirement began as a policy for people nearing the end of life – the aged – and in 1935, sixty-five was a reasonable age to choose. But longevity has altered the rules of the game. We need a corresponding shift in mindset that inserts a new phase into our work time line, one that occurs before we become aged (at who-knows-what age) and withdraw from work. Every day, thousands of employees leave the organizations in which they spent their final working years and move into retirement activities or Legacy Careers. They are the company's alumni. In some cases, companies find they have more alumni than active employees or, depending on the sector, more alumni than customers. Still, they must attract new employees to fill the positions left vacant.

Often, these organizations rely on their active employees as their only employee brand ambassadors. They may design programs to improve employees' skill as ambassadors or to incentivize current employees to scout for talent. But while the idea that only active employees make good brand ambassadors is a well-established belief, it is not grounded in fact.

Discussing with an employee when they will retire is awkward. Speculation about how long they still want to work may be useless. And opportunities for older workers to approach management with suggestions or requests regarding their transition into new roles are at best limited, and at worst futile. Meaningful career transitions in one's fifties, sixties, and seventies are not yet a part of normal discourse. Nor are they part of any formal talent structure. The challenge now is to normalize these transitions so they are expected chapters in every employee's career time line.

Employees can, of course, remain working for as long as they would like and as long as they are capable. But at some point, opportunities to change, to learn, and to grow become increasingly limited. Career stagnation sets in for no other reason than the current reality that neither organizations nor employees know how to find good, mutually beneficial options that are sustainable, scalable, and simple to implement – and they make no effort to find them.

Just as people are living longer, healthier, more productive lives, the employee life cycle is longer too, and because it is, employees fret about decreased corporate commitment to their careers. They struggle with the inadequacies of the overall structure of corporate career paths and, having found new opportunities in a freelance model, they are pursuing them. They've replaced traditional long-term career-path thinking with a short-term, transactional focus on what work needs to be done today. Among the many advantages they've discovered in this new world are tax and lifestyle benefits that derive from *not* being a permanent employee bound by the associated responsibilities. These employees may transition with purpose in the short to medium term into a new role that's very different from the role they currently hold and, contrary to what used to be, this sort of move is not seen negatively as job-hopping or a lack of career commitment, but positively as adaptive and market-responsive behavior. Right now, there is a sign posted in many Toronto subway cars. It is a Huron University College ad that reads: "The average career has ten jobs – I want an education for that." Educators, it seems, have their target audience nailed. It's time that companies did too.

Considering Legacy Careers an option for older workers requires a shift in mindset for leaders, yes, but it requires an equally major shift for employees. We are talking about a cohort that matured in the days of patriarchal organizations, a cohort that does not uniformly assume agency over their own careers – a generation that expects the employer to dictate their career paths even if, as individuals, they would have preferred it to be otherwise. That mindset will change when the company provides cues about possible next steps. Without cues, employees assume there are no next steps available to them. When options are available, employees make suitable choices for a meaningful and productive Legacy Career.

In 2014, Taylor met with a task force at one of Canada's largest banks to discuss how they were reinventing career management as they prepared for significant numbers of employees to retire. Their goal was to attract the right talent at all levels and they felt the strength of their employer brand would be key to their success.

Bank employees enjoy significant benefits throughout their working life. Many spend their entire career within "The Bank," identifying with its brand and being strong ambassadors for their workplace. The day an employee retires this longstanding relationship is abruptly severed. No longer an employee, a dedicated and highly knowledgeable resource instantly becomes just another customer, managed in the same way you might be managed if you opened your very first account with the bank today.

Big mistake! Indeed, for the next twenty years, organizations must rethink the phases of employee life cycle – that is, when it begins and when it ends. While there is an increased awareness that employer branding leads to better entry-level and on-campus recruitment results, the real power of your employer brand rests with your fifty-and-older workforce.

There is growing recognition of the value that corporate alumni communities bring to the organizations and brands that continue to recognize and foster their loyalty. In an era in which crowd-sourced opinion about organizations is available on Glassdoor.com, LinkedIn, and other such sites, it is utter foolishness to treat employees who know your organization intimately in the same way you treat ordinary customers, or worse still, not to consider them at all or fail to realize that they are an integral part of your ecosystem.

As careers extend well beyond the old definition of "working age," it becomes increasingly obvious that your alumni remain part of your overall talent equity long after they've cleaned out their desks. Even a quick glance at a few LinkedIn member profiles proves it. Savvy workers know the importance of capturing their own personal career-brand equity, and LinkedIn has become a lot more than a repository of résumés: it is a talent platform that has transformed recruitment and sales, among other business activities. It is also a testament to the ongoing value of your alumni because employee profiles publicly tie individuals to company brands – even brands in their distant past. For example, despite Taylor leaving Deloitte in 2000, she is still asked what it is like to work for the firm because audiences and conference participants have seen it listed in her profile. Despite leaving her practice of psychiatric occupational therapy in 1989, Lebo is still asked how to manage dysfunctional teams because people have read about her expertise on LinkedIn.

In the past, professional services and consulting organizations like McKinsey or Bain & Company have been recognized for their investment in maintaining strong links with their former employees through alumni networks. Their goal is to stay in contact with employees who have an attachment to the company in which they began their career, and to maintain contact with these former employees as they move into increasingly senior leadership roles in other organizations, where they become potential clients. A serious effort is made to ensure a strong affiliation with the corporate brand throughout a person's entire career and in return, companies receive value, support, and connection long after the employee's resignation.

The focus on alumni development and support has served these companies well. Former employees often move into leadership roles and their transition from employee to alumni imbues a sense of status that strengthens their loyalty and increases their future willingness to work as both provider and client.

There is an argument to be made that any organization with more than a thousand employees will see a strong return on investment when they create, foster, and grow an alumni community. Even in sectors in which the likelihood of an alum referring work back to the business is remote, there are strong indications that alumni with longstanding service within the organization can continue to enhance employer brand and address specific strategic needs across the organization's value chain.

Observations from the Field

Taylor works with a variety of talent-focused technology partners. Recently, she interviewed Tony Audino, President, Conzenza.

"The average tenure of employees around the world has been shortening, but with the emergence of the millennial generation it is even shorter. For example, Amazon is now estimating employee longevity at one year (median tenure). Because of this phenomenon there is an increased interest in alumni networks with five dominant value propositions depending on the company and sector," says Tony Audino, president of Conenza, a technology company focused on measuring and enabling alumni communities.

According to Audino, good alumni programs translate into real numbers. That is, 10 to 15 percent of new hires are recommended or referred by their alumni communities (known as boomerangs or referrals). Targets can be set and programs can be measured. Business planning can also rely on these activities.

In many cases, the alumni population is equal to or greater than employee population, which means that companies can double their network intelligence by including alumni in community and network mapping or strategy.

Action Steps for HR Leaders

Identify high-value, high-priority Legacy Career roles. Answer the following question:

1 If you had an employee who knew your brand, had a strong, existing network, and knew how to get things done within your company, where would this type of employee be most valuable?

2 Make a list of positions or roles that could benefit from this kind of talent. Note whether these opportunities are full time, part time, seasonal, flexible, etc. Categorize each role as delivering significant business value, moderate business value, or minimal business value.

3 For each of the roles or positions identified in step 1, determine what must be done to create the job and move someone into the role. What politics are involved? How much training is necessary? Determine whether creating that role is highly complex, moderately complex, or simple.

4 Gather your executive team and discuss the roles you've identified as high business value and simple to implement. Use these roles as a starting point to creating new Legacy Career paths within your company.

5 Expect career ownership from every employee at every age and stage and measure managers on the quality of their career conversations with employees of all ages. Proper career audit and assessment tools are available and their use can be tailored to the size and culture of your business. (See challengefactory.ca for additional resources and information.)

6 Teach employees to develop their own career criteria, which includes how work and extracurricular activities satisfy their needs, uses their inherent talents, focuses on their priorities, and make an impact needed in the market. Pursue discussions with employees to explore how these updated criteria align with roles your executive team has identified. Come to that discussion as equal parties because you have a variety of talent needs and the employee has defined career criteria and needs. Then find answers to the following questions: How can you both maximize your opportunities? What trade-offs might be required? Using a talent-equity approach, how will you each decide if the trade-off is worthwhile?

7 Provide self-management tools and support services throughout employees' working life to ensure they continue to evaluate

their career criteria and plan ahead for changes. Be certain they know that they'll remain in control of their own career choices as the world of work continues to shift over time.

8 Normalize the expectation that alumni remain part of your talent ecosystem.

9 Implement alumni programs to foster relationships that go beyond social events and community service projects. As part of the annual business planning cycle, identify which of your business priorities could benefit from alumni participation, and implement engagement initiatives to ensure alumni involvement. Typical priority areas might include: recruitment efforts, social media community building, crowdsourcing plant and equipment challenges seeking new solutions, skills training, project management support, or feedback/focus group communities.

> Employees are part of your talent equity (value) even after leaving your organization.

Key Points

- HR leaders share the responsibility of stepping into elevated roles; it's time for the CHRO to focus on culture.
- We are in a neutral zone vis-à-vis career models.
- Organizations need the right talent infrastructure to turn an aging workforce into a competitive advantage.
- Corporate values must be aligned with corporate communications.
- Intergenerational approaches spanning the full working-life continuum can lead to greater collaboration, efficiency, and innovation.
- Normalize Legacy Career paths.
- Consider alumni a valuable component of your talent equity.

12

CRITICAL ACTIONS FOR
FRONTLINE MANAGERS

You can shift strategic thinking and implement new operational models, but until your workforce changes in lock-step with the organization, there will be an internal dissonance that increases the resistance to change. When organizations make strategic changes at a faster pace than the workforce can absorb, myths and objections pop up everywhere. At every turn, there is suspicion and specula-tion, and a persistent dissemination of misinformation. Emotions run high and trust levels plummet.

If you are a frontline manager, you know you are the keeper of your company's culture and the guardian of your company's strategy. You have dozens of conversations that impact individual employee careers – sometimes conveying mixed messages and creating confusion if the information presented fails to align with other corporate messaging.

In our work, we often encounter a perplexed audience when we're asked to speak with employees about Legacy Careers. We know that skepticism is to be expected. Having been through years of downsizing, rightsizing, and outsourcing, employees do not trust the motives of a company initiative ostensibly designed to make retirement more meaningful. It sounds a lot like doublespeak. There is no good-faith record to give employees confidence. And as a stand-alone topic, employees would be right to suspect ulterior motives. After all, most organizations have been managing the workforce as assets – quick to offload those who are deemed "fully depreciated."

But these are not ordinary times. Your interest in new thinking about retirement is not about business as usual, but rather about transforming your workforce, beginning with your older workers. You want to capitalize on demographic change and be one of the winners in the talent revolution. It begins with clarity in everything – whether it be situational analysis or strategic planning. The foundation for any new relationship with your employees must be based on all the truths you've discovered throughout this book. There's no need to introduce new retirement workshops or programs, mentoring opportunities or knowledge champions until you have normalized a new type of relationship with your employees – one in which they have personal agency for their career, with the skills, authority, and confidence to take back control from the outdated and counterproductive career-pathing structures of the past.

Supercharge Your Workforce with Reliance on Frontline Managers

Frontline managers play a critical role in the talent revolution. Often, they are at a disadvantage because their information about future direction or strategies is incomplete. Yet, they have dozens of career-related conversations with employees every day, and every interaction is an opportunity for employees to glean valuable information about how management perceives their worth. Whether the conversation is a formal opportunity to discuss career options or a casual meeting at the water cooler, employees search for clues and interpret subtle messages – while the manager may be completely unaware of the impact their banter has on those under them.

We have found that many of the senior leaders inside organizations are cognizant of demographic shifts and consider longevity and aging a strategic issue. However, once we leave the upper echelons, we often find that mid-level and frontline managers have no more awareness of the key trends or emerging workforce models than the majority of employees do. In the main, managers' connection to HR is infrequent, and when they do engage, their discussions are usually focused on issues of compliance, training, performance-management issues, and employee relations. That must change. In an era when career paths and patterns are shifting, when outdated models are being revolutionized, it is critical to provide career-management education, training, and support for frontline managers.

Those organizations that are ready for the talent revolution develop managers who know why and how to hold career conversations (not performance discussions) with staff of all ages. At the C level, you know where emerging career opportunities are about to materialize for experienced staff, how to embed intergenerational learning opportunities in any role, and what specific business benefits managers will reap as a talent equity manager. You are intimately familiar with the five myths outlined in part 2 of this book, and you understand how to address them as they inevitably arise in both short-term and long-term planning. You are the frontline generals who must translate sound workforce strategy to the troops experiencing the greatest change – your experienced workers.

To build the kind of relationships required to lead the talent revolution, senior leadership must recognize your critical role and provide you with new tools. Remember that revolutions are chaotic and not everyone can envision how and when the next phase will emerge. But everyone knows how it feels to be caught in the midst of change and everyone needs the tools and support to help their teams navigate and emerge as winners – not casualties – of the revolution.

Supercharge Your Workforce by Training Managers to Identify Hidden Needs

Frontline managers know when the actions of the organization are not aligned with those of their team. But because they are not privy to backroom discussions and strategic decisions, they lack the context required to understand precisely what they are observing and sensing, and therefore may not be able to identify the exact cause of this disconnect. And yet, despite this lack of information, they are adept at navigating the gray zone to keep their teams performing in uncertain times – a critical skill during revolutions. In times of major change, CEOs and CHROs also suffer from a lack of information, context, and relationships. While they may know the long-term projections, strategies, risks, and rationales, they usually cannot know the impact, interpretation, and implications of the changes they initiate. Sites like Glassdoor.com have helped expose what employees really think about their leadership teams, corporate strategy, and workplace environment. Still, the complete picture remains unclear.

Observations from the Field

New artificial intelligence (AI) tools, such as Receptiviti.ai, combine machine learning and psychology to provide real-time information about employee engagement, behavior, and risks in ways that were never before possible. Receptivity.ai describes its mandate as follows: to "revolutionize the way CEOs and CHROs understand the mood, motivation, and mindset of their organizations. The solution utilizes Receptiviti's … AI, psychology, and linguistics platform to diagnose key factors influencing employee success. The existing method of measuring employee sentiment and experience relies solely on cumbersome surveys deployed once or twice per year. Now, CEOs and CHROs will be able to understand what is really going on in the organization in real time and without surveys. Having this kind of organizational intelligence enables key executives to implement leadership strategies that enhance performance" (Receptiviti Inc. 2018).

While it is true that AI can provide astounding insights, widespread adoption of these technologies is still in its early days. But change is coming – and while we await results frontline managers can play a significant role in helping us navigate.

While managers may not always know the causes or cures for the dissonance between corporate intention and the employee experience, they know immediately when that dissonance materializes. They hear it when messages are passed to them with a request to pass along to their teams. They sense it when an employee expresses a concern or view that reveals a misalignment with a critical value. They know when the disconnect occurs but may not know how to turn these occasions into opportunities for themselves, their teams, and their executives.

Recently, while working with a financial services firm, Taylor encountered a division manager who had decided to ban the use of the term "yeah, but" in any group discussion. In endeavoring to shift this organization's culture from one of change-resistance to one of risk and adventure, the leader had decided that language is powerful and that "yeah, but" would no longer be permitted as part of the dialogue. Instead, managers were encouraged to express their views

Observations from the Field

Here are a few examples of recent "yeah, buts" we have heard and how they reveal misunderstandings and untapped opportunities.

Yeah, but ...	I need ...	Actual result
This new work requires learning new technology and my older staff doesn't adapt well to change.	• To make sure everyone has access to training. • To find out how my staff learn best. • To make sure I explain why new tools are needed and how they improve our work. • To listen to concerns raised in case I have missed something important about the new technology.	Gap in training manual and process was identified, reducing training time by 50 percent.
The new position in my department is at a lower level with fewer direct reports than other positions. My existing older workers wouldn't be interested.	• A template or set of standard questions to ask during ongoing career conversations so I know what people value about their job. • To stop associating people-management with seniority. Some people want direct reports. Others want to focus on work without managing people. • To learn if there are skills my employees have that our talent management system doesn't capture. • To be supported and educated about what is and is not possible within our organization and according to employment law so I don't rely on assumptions.	Senior accountant moved to social media community manager based on skills gained in weekend volunteer work. Opened up position in accounting for younger staff and reengaged older worker as a brand advocate with direct client contact.
Sue used to be a great employee and now she is checked out and hard to work with.	• An alternative to waiting her out and hoping she quits. • To consider that something else might be going on with Sue. Maybe it isn't age. Maybe she's bored or dealing with something I should be able to help her with.	Provided environment where employee could share change in mental health status that had gone undiagnosed. Employee returned to high-performer status with renewed loyalty and connection to company.

using terms like "yes, and." This approach is quite common in coaching curricula because it encourages positive thinking.

In chapter 5 we introduced a technique to transform "yeah, but" reactions into essential feedback for those who are leading revolutionary change. Frontline managers can transform their awareness of dissonance into improved career conversations with staff and better feedback for leadership by recognizing that every "yeah, but" conceals needs that have not been identified, acknowledged, or addressed. When frontline managers express "yeah, buts" like those myths we addressed in part 2, we can get past misinformation and mistaken perception to provide real, actionable information that addresses managers' and employees' concerns and needs.

We call this "objection-based needs analysis," and when everything is changing simultaneously, managers' freedom to go with their "guts" often leads to simple, elegant, and powerful tools, conversations, and approaches.

Supercharge Your Workforce by Refusing to Allow Coasting as a Kindness

Managing employee performance is challenging for many managers. Regardless of how many times they've conducted a formal performance review or had a performance-related conversation, many managers, though they accept this part of their job as necessary, are not necessarily motivated by it. We know of many managers who feel it isn't appropriate to criticize the work of older workers, even when performance or attitude is an issue. The common theme in these cases is that there is little one can expect to change, that the conversation will only serve to upset both the employee and the employer, and that there is a risk of being accused of ageism, all of which makes the discussion difficult.

Chapter 8 illuminated why performance management should not be made dependent on age (when age is used as an excuse to overlook poor performance, it is a disservice to both the employer and the employee). When job performance declines – at any age – employers need to address this concern with the employee in question. Often, managers in organizations that do not provide performance-management tools, training, and support take a "path of least resistance" approach to performance. As long as the sub-standard performance does not impede department goals, it is left to slide in acknowledgment of years of service and in the hope that the employee will soon retire on their own anyway.

But in a talent revolution you need the full power of your workforce working for you – not against you. As a frontline manager, you must build the momentum that drives all of your staff to persist in developing their careers and skills. Given the whiplash speed of change today, nearly everyone will be facing job change in the next ten years. In fact, it is projected that in every existing role at least 30 percent of current work will be replaced by automation by 2030. Now is not the time for you to be a passive manager. Nor is it the time for your employees to be passive. Coasting is not a kindness. It is a sign that you have counted the employee out. Moreover, it indicates an employee and an organization that will not navigate smoothly into the new world of work.

Action Steps for Managers

1 Identify who should be a part of your "frontline and mid-manager" community of revolutionaries and trailblazers.
2 From this group, assess who has demonstrated an aptitude for translating strategic change into day-to-day action that employees can understand and accept. Engage these leaders to help you build your company's talent revolution toolkit.

3 Provide education to all employees on workforce trends
   (perhaps sharing a copy of this book to guide the learning) and
   the implications for your specific one- to five-year workforce
   plans. Challenge outdated assumptions and be sure you address
   the "yeah, buts" that are raised. Ensure every manager understands the fallacies represented by the five myths.
4 Review your annual workforce planning processes to identify
   where ageism has crept into common practice. Identify tools
   for managers to address performance-based issues. Provide a
   different set of tools for managers to use to foster good Legacy
   Career conversations among employees of all ages. What might
   they want to contribute in their fifties, sixties, and seventies?
   By starting these conversations early, managers can start
   normalizing Legacy Career paths and establish new and
   appropriate working-life expectancies among employees.
5 Consider career-management and career-development tools,
   approaches, and training for your managers. Recognizing that
   career paths are now less linear than ever before, and ensuring your
   managers are exceptional career managers, is a smart investment.

Key Points

- Frontline managers play a critical role and need career development education, tools, and opportunities.
- Learning how to listen for objections (or "yeah, buts") will create
  opportunities to understand employee needs and address
  workforce issues with creativity and grace.
- Knowing how to have career and performance conversations is a
  critical management skill and should be one that is exercised with
  employees of all ages, even when these discussions are difficult.

13

FROM THE TALENT REVOLUTION
TO THE FUTURE OF WORK

Since 1935, when sixty-two was the average length of life and sixty-five was established as a reasonable retirement age, twenty years have been added to the average life span. Still, attitudes about aging have changed little in the more than eight decades since. In short, older people get a bad rap. That's why we're calling for you to join the talent revolution – so everybody wins.

The configuration of your talent pool has changed, and in this book we have focused on age and longevity. We have explored its impact in the workplace and made a business case for taking advantage of the wisdom and skill already on the payroll. We have looked briefly at the research of social psychologists who explain the inferential rules people tend to use to make judgments (Kunda 1999) and predict behaviors for entire groups with little concern for reality, and we have exploded the five major myths that stem from negative stereotypes about aging workers. We contend that in the workplace, as in other areas of life, stereotypes damage everyone by suffocating the symbiosis essential to an organization's performance, interfering with individual agency and self-actualization, and thwarting the organization's ability to achieve the ideal state. In addition to making the case for joining the revolution, we've provided guidance for flipping objections into actions, and we created a roadmap for turning your aging workforce into a competitive advantage.

We know the aging workforce is only one dynamic currently shaping the future of work, which is why we began by zooming out to examine five drivers that all CEOs, CHROs, and managers must acknowledge as work continues to change. Longevity has led to longer working lives and the resulting talent revolution provides a new way to look at your changing workforce. Further, we have described new models and approaches to help employers and employees adapt not only to changing conditions vis-à-vis aging in the workplace, but also to the shifting nature of work across all five drivers.

When older workers thrive in their existing organizations, when they are included, motivated, and empowered, they can take increased ownership of their own careers. Stepping out from behind formal career path structures and employer-driven career models, older employees can evaluate their own career criteria at this stage of their life, and identify alternative paths that better suit their needs. Today, older workers are defining new relationships between themselves and their employer. They are seeking new roles "in retirement," shifting careers from one field to another, contributing in myriad ways – inside their organizations or out. Unfortunately, it is still typical to see people leave their organizations before making a shift first into retirement, then into working somewhere else. While sometimes this arrangement is to everyone's advantage, too often organizations miss out on the opportunity to capitalize on lifelong talent equity.

As career ownership models evolve, and as the number of role models from whom older workers can learn increases, we predict we will continue to see a rise in participation rates in the freelance economy – the third driver. Youth is not a requirement for participating or thriving in the freelance economy. But success does require skill development, a supportive community, and a new understanding of individual value. Alternative working models offer a number of real benefits and it's no wonder platforms that help older workers find freelance "gigs" are oversubscribed with far greater numbers of consultants registering for participation than employers needing them. We predict these conditions will reach a balance in coming years as Legacy Careers become normalized.

We assert that new platform-based business models will also benefit from the increased participation of older workers. There, relationships are king and the goal is to amplify the success of other people's products and services. Platforms are complex business models, where the underlying technology that connects buyers and sellers is but a small component of what drives competitive advantage. Nuance, industry understanding, partnership models, relationship skills, and intuition play a large role in defining the next Uber, Airbnb, or Alibaba.

Which leads us to the final driver – AI and robotics. For this driver we take a long-term view and explore how technology will continue to evolve to create new roles, work, and needs well past 2030. Here, too, our older workers hold unique keys of understanding. As they navigate unprecedented workplace challenges and adjust the ways in which they internalize work, worth, value, and contribution – at the time they once anticipated withdrawing from working life – boomers can provide a blueprint for how to find a meaningful next role. Of course, the transition is not smooth – or equal. There are older workers in certain professions, jobs, and geographies that are at a clear disadvantage. The way organizations, government, and society react to the growing boomer population needing or wanting work will also establish patterns that can serve as guideposts for intervention, transition, and support for workers of all ages who find themselves needing or wanting to make changes, sometimes under difficult circumstances or as the result of technological advancement.

Organizations that embrace the permanent shift in working-life expectancy and capitalize on the opportunities it presents will also demonstrate the required cultural, strategic, and operational acumen to move smoothly into the future.

Culture changes when there is a clear shift in values – one revealed in behaviors, policies, procedures, and practices. Imagine the assumptions that could be challenged and the innovations that could be unleashed if everyone within your organization understood that current employment relationships have the potential to deliver a lifelong ROI as people move into new roles within your organization, or even as retirees or alumni. Equally important, as a society we must acknowledge the prevalence of ageism and commit to calling it out whenever it surfaces. We cannot hope to live up to the potential that longevity promises if we start discounting experience and abilities in our forties and fifties. Nor can we profit from the potential that longevity promises if mature workers are sidelined, overlooked, or counseled out.

Strategic transformation occurs when order is brought to chaos. That order becomes evident when employees and leaders feel there is a path forward – in their own career and for the organization – and it requires a breadth of new approaches. Implementing new approaches to career pathing means including roles for the Legacy

Career phase as well as incorporating meaningful alumni programs. These approaches serve to separate the chronic issues facing an aging workforce from urgent, acute workforce issues such as immediate skill shortages or shallow leadership candidate pools. When new approaches to career pathing are established, resources are more effectively allocated and older workers become part of the long-term solution in sustainable, mutually beneficial ways.

Operational improvements are realized when cultural and strategic changes take hold and impact day-to-day discussions and decisions. The talent revolution should ignite new and different conversations for individuals who are navigating work, life, and their own career potential. Forget the platitudes. Employees and managers need practical tools to challenge deeply ingrained myths and to prepare for meaningful career development.

Leadership is not a spectator sport. Everyone in your employ – regardless of age or demographic cohort – must be held to the same standards and given the same opportunities. Longevity is your single greatest competitive opportunity. To profit from the untapped source of wealth within your ranks, it's time to grab the reins and lead.

ACKNOWLEDGMENTS

This book has been influenced by many people. Some might recognize their contribution as they read these pages. Others might not realize the significant impact of their actions, words, and friendship. I will try to acknowledge all that have been a part of this book's journey, whether they knew it or not – and will likely fail. If you are reading this and feel slighted that I did not mention you – please know that it was an honest oversight and entirely my fault. I'll make it up to you.

This book would not have come together without my coauthor, Fern Lebo, who remained ever realistic and committed to turning abstract ideas into a book that is insightful and action-focused. Tim Casswell and Jennifer LaTrobe were our earliest readers, and, thanks to Tim's artistic talents, they brought creativity to the text. Fern and I were also fortunate to be supported by our terrific students, including Nev Balendra, Ben Martin, Alexandra Tashos, Lucrezia Rampinini, and Silvia Riva.

In my early career I was supported by many brilliant academics and corporate leaders. Dr. C.E.S. (Ned) Franks introduced me to research and invited me into a select group of assistants he affectionately called "Urchins." He died on 11 September 2018 and leaves a remarkable legacy. Dr. Jonathan Rose, Dr. Matthew Mendelsohn, Dr. Dezsö J. Horváth, Dr. Ellen Auster, Dr. Patricia Bradshaw, Dr. Ian Macdonald, Dr. Allan Middleton, and Dr. Theodore Peridis taught me the value of an interdisciplinary mindset. Raymond Pineda, Mario Vitale, Edward Wong, and Michael Ianni-Palarchio gave me tools to tackle complex client projects. Lynn Jones, Nicole Matta, and Jackie Parker pushed me to lead larger teams and take on greater responsibilities.

I thank those who supported me as I left corporate life to launch Challenge Factory – especially Igor Samuk, John Tikins, Wayne Stark, Cameron Shouldice, Brad Elberg, Gareth Edwards (who created Challenge Factory's first logo and has never been properly acknowledged), and Patti Edwards. Thank you for listening and encouraging me in those early days.

I have been so fortunate to have amazing colleagues at Challenge Factory, including Cayla Charles (who makes everything possible), Michael Ehling, Candice Pascal van Alphen, Wayne Pagani, Stephanie Clark, Valarie Rayner, Andy Marchant, Jill Jukes, Maureen McCann, and Nel Slater.

Business Connections One group members were and are also incredibly special. It was at a group meeting one cold, dark morning that the Broken Talent Escalator analogy was first revealed. I especially thank Rona Birenbaum, Jim Stewart, James Minns, Paul Chato, Ian Young, Katie Tingley, Mark Bowden, Tracey Thompson, Janine Harris, Dan Trommater, Ian Young, Andrew Jenkins, Jeremy Miller, Kate Erickson, Chris Case, and Laurelea Conrad.

Partners and clients I am proud to call friends advanced the thinking and content of this book in so many ways. I am grateful to Dr. Nasreen Khatri, Priya Bates, Suzanne Filiatrault, Sharon Graham, Judy Fantham, Emree Siaroff, Larry Meyers, Adrianna Ico, Lisa Wilkins, Kim Buote, Margaret Parent, Trevor Buttrum, Heather Rose, Don Edmonds, Russel Baskin, Peter Vondracek, Marjorie Brans, Brina Ludwig-Prout, Soula Courlas, Dr. Maureen MacDonald, Ronna Rubin, Sandra Kerr, Elaine Lam, and Katie Ochin. I also thank Bob Berube and Karine Lachappelle for introducing me to the Canadian Special Operations Forces community, including Leen Bolle, Roman Hrycyna, and Brett Nesbitt. I owe much to you all for your service and have learned a great deal about careers, identity, and transitions from our discussions.

Formal and informal advisors have provided kind criticism while pushing me to think bigger. I thank Dr. Marie Bountrogianni, Dr. Maurice Bitran, Simon North, Scott Bissessar, Anne Golden (OC) (who was an early reader who provided helpful feedback), Michael Nicin, Kevin Press, Keka DasGupta, Riz Ibrahim, Sharon Graham, Jim Emmerman, Betsy Werley, Dr. Lianne Trachtenberg, Raf Choudhury, and Rob Besner (who always seems to recommend the right book at the right time).

Bringing a book into the world is a whole-life activity, and my friends have been part of every step along the way; this includes Rabbi Yael Splanksy, Ann Lamont, Janet Cloud, Sue Folinsbee, Stephanie MacKendrick, Angela Mitchell, and Dr. Joel and Shelley Kirsh (whose hospitality at Birch Grove provided the ideal setting for the completion of the last chapter in the good company of Eric and Deborah Beutel). There are many, many others who listened, provided coffee, and helped with car pools. Thanks to you all.

Family is the easiest and hardest to thank. None of my career shifts would have been possible without the unconditional support of my father, Les Rothschild. He is my greatest champion and strongest critic. In true intergenerational fashion, it is a joy to work together every chance we get – which, fortunately, is often. My mother, Bev Rothschild, provides the love and support needed for me to portray the illusion that I can actually "do it all." My husband Christian has been by my side since we were teens, and I wouldn't have it any other way. Together we are raising two teens of our own who amaze me every day with their kindness, compassion, humor, and intelligence. Hayden is the best VP of marketing Challenge Factory has ever had, and Ethan keeps a keen eye open for international opportunities that just might need to be explored in person.

This book was written at CSI-Annex, in coffee shops, on the ledge at Verity Club, at Baseline Sports, on bleachers at various baseball parks across Ontario, at friends' cottages, in the Locketz's kitchen in Minnesota, and on the balcony of The Barclay in Florida. Regardless of where I was, Justin Bieber tunes seemed to provide the perfect background to keep my thoughts and words flowing – so thanks to Justin too.

My final thanks are for my sister, Debbie Locketz. You are my person.

– Lisa Taylor

Special thanks to Lisa, whose wisdom, indefatigable spirit, and original thinking were the impetus for this book. Happily, Lisa was a joy to work with. I am also indebted to our wonderful students: Nev Balendra, Ben Martin, Alexandra Tashos, Lucrezia Rampinini, and Silvia Riva.

I am especially grateful to my husband Alan Brudner, the finest writer I know. He is my life partner, my dearest support, and my greatest champion. His keen eye, love of language, and gentle nudge keep my writing crisp. Thanks, too, to my sons Bram, Matthew, and Jay, for their helpful feedback and perceptive insights, and to my sister Joyce, for her wisdom and calming influence. And thanks to Lewis Eisen for his valuable input.

Thanks to my clients who graciously allowed me to tell their stories. While I have changed their names out of respect for their privacy, I am sincerely grateful for their openness and willingness to share. Thanks are also due to my first publisher, Malcolm Lester, who guided me through my early books and taught me the importance of disciplined writing. Everyone should have a first publisher like Malcolm.

And finally, I would be remiss if I neglected to acknowledge those wonderful clients who mentored me over the years. Among them: Dave Holley of HP, the first to hire me, who taught me the importance of knowing your audience, and who kept me on the sales-training team for fifteen years; Ron Marriott, who championed me and took me with him wherever he went; Karen Pettoruto of Philips, who supported me and opened many doors; and Anita Lieberman of Sun Life and Desjardins, who valued candor and opened my eyes to ageism within the organization.

I am grateful to you all.

– Fern Lebo

REFERENCES

1 The Future of Work and the Talent Revolution

BlessingWhite Research. (2013). *Employee engagement research report.* Retrieved from http://blessingwhite.com/research-report/2013/01/01/employee-engagement-research-report-update-jan-2013/

Future of Life Institute. (2017). "Implications of AI for the economy and society." Retrieved from https://www.youtube.com/watch?v=CyfI_8ucZPA&t=1033s

James, J.B., S. McKechnie, and J. Swanberg. (2011). "Predicting employee engagement in an age-diverse retail workforce." *Journal of Organizational Behavior,* 32(2), 173–96. https://doi.org/10.1002/job.681

Kite, M.E., G.D. Stockdale, B.E. Whitley, and B.T. Johnson. (2005). "Attitudes toward younger and older adults: An updated meta-analytic review." *Journal of Social Issues,* 61(2), 241–66. https://doi.org/10.1111/j.1540-4560.2005.00404.x

McCarthy, J., N. Heraty, C. Cross, and J.N. Cleveland. (2014). "Who is considered an 'older worker'? Extending our conceptualisation of 'older' from an organisational decision maker perspective." *Human Resource Management Journal,* 24(4), 374–93. https://doi.org/10.1111/1748-8583.12041

Smith, A. (2014). "Older adults and technology use: Adoption is increasing, but many seniors remain isolated from digital life." Pew Research Center.

Taylor, L. (2017). "Planning for the future of work: Lessons from the chronic to acute and back again." Retrieved from https://www.challengefactory.ca/chronicandacute

World Economic Forum. (2018a). "Are you ready for the technological revolution?" Retrieved from https://www.weforum.org/agenda/2015/02/are-you-ready-for-the-technological-revolution/

World Economic Forum. (2018b). "Preparing for the future of work." Retrieved from https://www.weforum.org/projects/future-of-work

2 A Social Revolutionary Lens: Welcome to the Revolution

Aberle, D.F. (1966). "A classification of social movements. The peyote religion among the Navaho." *Viking Fund Publications in Anthropology* (42), 315–33.

Baruch, Y. (2004). "Transforming careers: From linear to multidirectional career paths." *Career Development International*, 9(1), 58–73. https://doi.org/10.1108/13620430410518147

Bernard, A. (2012). "The job search of the older unemployed." Statistics Canada, 22 August. Retrieved from https://www150.statcan.gc.ca/n1/en/pub/75-001-x/2012003/article/11698-eng.pdf?st=4_46Fi1x

Challenge Factory and Creative Connection. (2018). "National Conversation on the Future of Work held at Cannexus18." Retrieved from www.challengefactory.ca/nationalconversation

Cook, S. L. (2013). Redirection: An extension of career during retirement. *The Gerontologist*, 55(3), 360–73. https://doi.org/10.1093/geront/gnt105

Cook, S.L., and V. Rougette. (2017). "Talent management and older workers: Later life career development." In *Ageing, Organisations and Management*, edited by Iiris Aaltio, Albert J. Mills, and Jean Helms Mill, 113–40. London: Palgrave Macmillan. https://doi.org/10.1007/978-3-319-58813-1_6

Crozier, M. (1972). "The relationship between micro and macrosociology: A study of organizational systems as an empirical approach to the problems of macrosociology." *Human Relations*, 25(3), 239–51. https://doi.org/10.1177/001872677202500304

Deloitte Consulting LLP and Bersin by Deloitte. (2014). "Global human capital trends 2014: Engaging the 21st century workforce." Retrieved from https://www2.deloitte.com/content/dam/Deloitte/ar/Documents/human-capital/arg_hc_global-human-capital-trends-2014_09062014%20(1).pdf

Dickson, R.G.B., J. Beetz, W.R. McIntyre, J. Chouinard, B. Wilson, G.E. Le Dain, and G.V. La Forest. (1987). *Reference re Public Service Employee Relations Act (Alta.)*. Retrieved from https://scc-csc.lexum.com/scc-csc/scc-csc/en/item/205/index.do

Frey, C.B., and M.A. Osborne. (2013). "The Future of Employment: How susceptible are jobs to computerisation?" Oxford Martin School/University of Oxford Working Paper. Retrieved from https://www.oxfordmartin.ox.ac.uk/downloads/academic/future-of-employment.pdf

Future of Life Institute. (2017). Robotics, AI, and the macro-economy: Jeffrey Sachs." Retrieved from https://www.youtube.com/watch?v=d8tlyFOq2tU&t=489s

Gurr, T. (1973). "The revolution, social-change nexus: Some old theories and new hypotheses." *Comparative Politics*, 5(3), 359–92. doi:10.2307/421270

Jensen, D.G. (1999). "The concept of 'ME Inc.' " *American Association for the Advancement of Science*. Retrieved from http://www.sciencemag.org/careers/1999/06/concept-me-incZ

Lyons, S., and L. Kuron. (2013). "Generational differences in the workplace: A review of the evidence and directions for future research." *Journal of Organizational Behavior*, 35(S1), S139–S157. https://doi.org/10.1002/job.1913

Lyons, S., L. Schweitzer, E.S.W. Ng, and L.K.J. Kuron. (2012). "Comparing apples to apples: A qualitative investigation of career mobility patterns across four generations." *Career Development International*, 17(4), 333–57. https://doi.org/10.1108/13620431211255824

Marist Poll. (2018). "NPR/Marist Poll results January 2018: Picture of work." Retrieved from http://maristpoll.marist.edu/nprmarist-poll-results-january-2018-picture-of-work/#sthash.JDmjTOyw.dpbs

Mitchell, M.C., and J.C. Murray. (2016). *Changing workplace review: Special advisors' interim report*. Toronto: Ontario Ministry of Labour. Retrieved from https://www.labour.gov.on.ca/english/about/pdf/cwr_interim.pdf

Munnell, A.., and W. Yanyuan. (2012). *Will delayed retirement by the baby boomers lead to higher unemployment among young workers?* Chestnut Hill, MA: Center for Retirement Research at Boston College.

Ozkal, D. (2016). "Millennials can't keep up with boomer entrepreneurs." *Ewing Marion Kauffman Foundation* (blog), 19 July. Retrieved from http://www.kauffman.org/blogs/growthology/2016/07/age-and-entrepreneurship

Pettey, C. (2015). "The internet of things is a revolution waiting to happen." Retrieved from http://www.gartner.com/smarterwithgartner/the-internet-of-things-is-a-revolution-waiting-to-happen/

Rahim, M.A., R.T. Golembiewski, and K.D.Mackenzie. (2003). *Current Topics in Management* (Vol. 8). New Brunswick, NJ: Transaction Publishers.

Rashid, B. (2016). "The rise of the freelancer economy." *Forbes*, 26 January. Retrieved from http://www.forbes.com/sites/brianrashid/2016/01/26/the-rise-of-the-freelancer-economy/#6308e540379a

Schwab, K. (2016). *The fourth industrial revolution*. Geneva: World Economic Forum.

Spokus, D.M. (2008). "Factors influencing older worker quality of life and intent to continue to work." PhD diss., Pennsylvania State University. Retrieved from https://eric.ed.gov/?id=ED527396

Stanton, B. (2000). "Y2K – Was It Worth It?" *Australian Journal of Emergency Management*, 15(2). Retrieved from https://search.informit.com.au/documentSummary;dn=369137200809365;res=IELHSS

The Economic Mobility Project. (2012). "When baby boomers delay retirement, do younger workers suffer?" *The PEW Charitable Trusts*. Retrieved
from http://www.pewtrusts.org/~/media/legacy/uploadedfiles/pcs_
assets/2012/empretirementdelaypdf.pdf

The Economist. (2014). "The third great wave." *The Economist: Special Report*,
4 October. Retrieved from https://www.economist.com/sites/default/
files/20141004_world_economy.pdf

Toffler, A. (1990). *Future shock*. New York: Bantam Books.

US Bureau of Labor Statistics. (2017). "Independent contractors made up 6.9
percent of employment in May 2017." *TED: The Economics Daily*, 21 June.
Retrieved from https://www.bls.gov/opub/ted/2018/independent-
contractors-made-up-6-point-9-percent-of-employment-in-may-2017.htm

Willis Towers Watson. (2016). "Global benefit attitudes survey 2015/2016."
Retrieved from https://www.willistowerswatson.com/en/
insights/2016/02/global-benefit-attitudes-survey-2015-16

Zizys, T. (2011). *Working better: Creating a high-performing labour
market in Ontario*. Toronto: *Metcalf Foundation*. Retrieved
from http://metcalffoundation.com/stories/publications/
working-better-creating-a-high-performing-labour-market-in-ontario-2/

3 A Career and Work Lens: Boomers as Revolutionaries

Applewhite, A. (2016). *This chair rocks: A manifesto against ageism*. New York:
Networked Books.

Bersin, J. (2012). "Building the borderless and agile workplace." *Bersin &
Associates*. Retrieved from https://docplayer.net/1009522-Building-the-
borderless-and-agile-workplace.html

Brownell, P., and R.P. Resnick. (2005). Intergenerational-multigenerational
relationships: Are they synonymous? *Journal of Intergenerational
Relationships*, 3(1), 67–75. https://doi.org/10.1300/j194v03n01_06

Burtless, G. (2013). "The impact of population aging and delayed retirement
on workforce productivity." The Centre for Retirement Research at Boston
College. https://doi.org10.2139/ssrn.2275023

Business Development Bank of Canada. (2013). "Managing an aging workforce – your business can respond." Retrieved from https://www.bdc.ca/
en/articles-tools/employees/manage/pages/boomers-business.aspx

Cappelli, P. (2014). "Engaging your older workers." *Harvard Business
Review*, 5 November. Retrieved from https://hbr.org/2014/11/
engaging-your-older-workers

Cohn, D., and P. Taylor. (2010). "Baby boomers approach 65 – glumly." *Pew Research Centre*. Retrieved from http://www.pewsocialtrends. org/2010/12/20/baby-boomers-approach-65-glumly/

Cook, S.L. (2013). "Redirection: An extension of career during retirement. *The Gerontologist*, 55(3), 360–73. https://doi.org/10.1093/geront/gnt105

Cook, S.L., and V. Rougette. (2017). "Talent management and older workers: Later life career development. In *Ageing, Organisations and Management*, edited by Iiris Aaltio, Albert J. Mills, and Jean Helms Mill, 113–40. London: Palgrave Macmillan. https://doi. org/10.1007/978-3-319-58813-1_6

Encore.org. (2017). "Higher Education – Innovative Encore Programs." Retrieved from https://encore.org/higher-education/

Freedman, M. (2011). *The big shift*. New York: Perseus Book Group.

Greenhouse, S. (2014). "The age of premium: Retaining older workers." *New York Times*, 14 May. Retrieved from https://www.nytimes. com/2014/05/15/business/retirementspecial/the-age-premium-retaining-older-workers.html?_r=0

Hedge, J.W., W.C. Borman, and S.E. Lammlein. (2006). *The aging workforce: Realities, myths, and implications for organizations*. Washington, DC: American Psychological Association.

Inc. (2015). "Inc. 5000 2015: The full list." Retrieved from http://www.inc. com/inc5000/list/2015/

Kanter, R.M. (2011). "Zoom in, zoom out." *Harvard Business Review*, 89(3), 112–6.

Loehr, A. (2016). "Why your company needs to stop recruiting 'digital natives.' " *Fast Company*. Retrieved from https://www.fastcompany. com/3059834/the-not-so-hidden-age-bias-in-recruiting-digital-natives

Lyons, S., and L. Schweitzer. (2016). "A qualitative exploration of generational identity: Making sense of young and old in the context of today's workplace." *Work, Aging and Retirement*, 3(2), 209–24. https://doi.org/10.1093/ workar/waw024

Ng, E.S., L. Schweitzer, and S.T. Lyons. (2010). "New generation, great expectations: A field study of the millennial generation." *Journal of Business and Psychology*, 25(2), 281–92. https://doi.org/10.1007/s10869-010-9159-4

Paullin, C. (2014). *The aging workforce: Leveraging the talents of mature employees*. Alexandria, VA: SHRM Foundation.

Schwab, K. (2016). *The fourth industrial revolution*. Geneva: World Economic Forum.

Sloan Centre for Aging and Work. (2008). "Innovating practices database." Retrieved from http://capricorn.bc.edu/agingandwork/database/ browse/case_study/24038

Society for Human Resource Management. (2015). "SHRM survey finding: The aging workforce – recruitment and retention." Retrieved from https://www.shrm.org/hr-today/trends-and-forecasting/research-and-surveys/pages/shrm-older-workers-recruitment-and-retention.aspx

Statistics Canada. (2014). "Portraits of Canada's labour force." Retrieved from http://www12.statcan.gc.ca/nhs-enm/2011/as-sa/99-012-x/99-012-x2011002-eng.cfm

Super, D.E. (1980). "A life-span, life-space approach to career development." *Journal of Vocational Behavior*, 16(3), 282–98.

Taylor, L. (2017a). "Planning for the future of work: Lessons from the chronic to acute and back again." Retrieved from https://www.challengefactory.ca/chronicandacute

Taylor, L. (2017b). *Retain and gain: Career management for small business.* Toronto: Canadian Education and Research Institute for Counselling.

United States Congress. (1985). *The congressional record.* Washington, DC: US Government Printing Office.

Van Dalen, H.P., K. Henkens, and J. Schippers. (2010). "Productivity of older workers: Perceptions of employers and employees. *Population and Development Review*, 36(2), 309–30. https://doi.org/10.1111/j.1728-4457.2010.00331.x

4 An Organizational Lens: The Broken Talent Escalator

Adkins, A. (2016). "Millennials: The job-hopping generation." *Gallup Business Journal*. Retrieved from http://www.gallup.com/businessjournal/191459/millennials-job-hopping-generation.aspx

Applewhite, A. (2016). "You're how old? We'll be in touch." *New York Times*, 3 September. Retrieved from https://www.nytimes.com/2016/09/04/opinion/sunday/youre-how-old-well-be-in-touch.html?_r=0

Bishop, M. (2016). *Economics: an A–Z guide.* London: Profile Books.

CERIC. (2016). "Guiding principles of career development." Retrieved from http://ceric.ca/guiding-principles-of-career-development/

Cook, S.L., and V. Rougette. (2017). "Talent management and older workers: Later life career development." In *Ageing, Organisations and Management*, edited by Iiris Aaltio, Albert J. Mills, and Jean Helms Mill, 113–40. London: Palgrave Macmillan. https://doi.org/10.1007/978-3-319-58813-1_6

Delsen, L., and G. Reday-Mulvey. (1996). *Gradual retirement in the OECD countries: Macro and micro issues and policies.* London: Dartmouth Publishing.

Lyons, S., and L. Kuron. (2014). "Generational differences in the workplace: A review of the evidence and directions for future research." *Journal of Organizational Behavior*, 35(S1), S139–S157. https://doi.org/10.1002/job.1913

Lyons, S., L. Schweitzer, E.S.W. Ng, and L.K.J. Kuron. (2012). "Comparing apples to apples: A qualitative investigation of career mobility patterns across four generations." *Career Development International*, 17(4), 333–57. https://doi.org/10.1108/13620431211255824

Meister, J. (2012). "The future of work: Job hopping is the 'new normal' for millennials." *Forbes*, 14 August. Retrieved from http://www.forbes.com/sites/jeannemeister/2012/08/14/the-future-of-work-job-hopping-is-the-new-normal-for-millennials/#f6ed477322df

Meister, J. (2013). "The boomer-millennial workplace clash: Is it real?" *Forbes*, 4 June. Retrieved from http://www.forbes.com/sites/jeannemeister/2013/06/04/the-boomer-millennial-workplace-clash-is-it-real/#10bbc04cd895

Society for Human Resource Management. (2007). "2007 change management: Survey report." Retrieved from https://www.shrm.org/hr-today/trends-and-forecasting/research-and-surveys/documents/2007%20change%20management%20survey%20report.pdf

The Economist. (2012). "Keep on trucking: Why the old should not make way for the young." *The Economist*, 11 February. Retrieved from http://www.economist.com/node/21547263

US Bureau of Labor Statistics. (2016). "New release: Employee tenure in 2016." Retrieved from https://www.bls.gov/news.release/pdf/tenure.pdf

US Bureau of Labor Statistics. (2018). "New release: Employee tenure summary." Retrieved from https://www.bls.gov/news.release/tenure.nr0.htm

5 From Theory to Practice: The Costs of Myths and Untruths

Berger, J. (2014). "Word of mouth and interpersonal communication: A review and directions for future research. *Journal of Consumer Psychology*, 24(4), 586–607. https://doi.org/10.1016/j.jcps.2014.05.002

Kunda, Z. (1999). *Social cognition: Making sense of people*. Cambridge, MA: MIT Press.

Paikin, S. (2017). "The fight against fake news." Presentation at Holy Blossom Temple, Toronto, 6 December 2017.

Schwarz, N., E. Newman, and W. Leach. (2016). "Making the truth stick &
the myths fade: Lessons from cognitive psychology." *Behavioral Science &
Policy*, 2(1), 85–95. https://doi.org/10.1353/bsp.2016.0009

6 Money Myths

Alon-Shenker, P. (2014). "Nonhiring and dismissal of senior workers: Is it all
about the money?" *Comparative Labor Law & Policy Journal*, 35(2). Retrieved
from https://ssrn.com/abstract=2386382
Brooke, L. (2003). "Human resource costs and benefits of maintaining a
mature-age workforce." *International Journal of Manpower*, 24(3), 260–83.
https://doi.org/10.1108/01437720310479732
Carstairs, S., and W.J. Keon. (2009). "Canada's aging population: Seizing
the opportunity." Retrieved from http://epe.lac-bac.gc.ca/100/200/301/
senate-senat/cttee_reports/aging/canadas_aging_population-ef/YC2-402-
3-01E.pdf
Deloitte Touche Tohmatsu. (2016). *The 2016 Deloitte millennial survey: Winning
over the next generation of leaders*. Retrieved from https://www2.deloitte.
com/content/dam/Deloitte/global/Documents/About-Deloitte/gx-
millenial-survey-2016-exec-summary.pdf
Families and Work Institute. (n.d.). "Older employees in the workforce:
A companion piece to generation and gender in the workplace." *American
Business Collaboration*. Retrieved from http://www.abcdependentcare.com/
docs/older-employees-in-the-workforce.pdf
Guvenen, F., F. KarAhan, S. Ozkan, and J. Song. (2015). "What do data on
millions of US workers reveal about life-cycle earnings risk?" *National
Bureau of Economic Research*.
Hewitt, A. (2015). "A business case for workers age 50+: A look at the value
of experience." *AARP Research*. Retrieved from http://states.aarp.org/wp-
content/uploads/2015/08/A-Business-Case-for-Older-Workers-Age-50-A-
Look-at-the-Value-of-Experience.pdf
Kitroeff, N. (2016). "Have millennials made quitting more common?"
Bloomberg, 12 February. Retrieved from http://www.bloomberg.com/
news/articles/2016-02-12/have-millennials-made-quitting-more-common
Knowledge@Wharton. (2010). "The 'Silver Tsunami': Why older workers
offer better value than younger ones." Wharton School of the University
of Pennsylvania. Retrieved from http://knowledge.wharton.upenn.edu/
article/the-silver-tsunami-why-older-workers-offer-better-value-than-
younger-ones/

McCarthy, J., N. Heraty, C. Cross, and J.N. Cleveland. (2014). "Who is considered an 'older worker'? Extending our conceptualisation of 'older' from an organisational decision maker perspective." *Human Resource Management Journal*, 24(4), 374–93. https://doi.org/10.1111/1748-8583.12041

Reade, N. (2013). "The surprising truth about older workers: Myths and perceptions." *AARP The Magazine*. Retrieved from www.aarp.org/work/job-hunting/info-07-2013/older-workers-more-valuable

Rothwell, W.J., H. Sterns, Diane Spokus, and Joel M. Reaser. (2008). *Working longer: New strategies for managing, training, and retaining older employees*. New York: AMACOM Books.

Rudgard, O. (2015). "Older workers healthier and more reliable." *Telegraph (London), 14 May*. Retrieved from http://www.telegraph.co.uk/news/health/news/11602715/Older-workers-healthier-and-more-reliable.html

US Bureau of Labor Statistics. (2016). "Employee tenure in 2016." Retrieved from https://www.bls.gov/news.release/pdf/tenure.pdf

Van Dalen, H.P., K. Henkens, and J. Schippers. (2010). "Productivity of older workers: Perceptions of employers and employees." *Population and Development Review*, 36(2), 309–30. https://doi.org/10.1111/j.1728-4457.2010.00331.x

7 Peak Performance Myths

Buyens, D., H. van Dijk, T. Dewilde, and A. De Vos. (2009). "The aging workforce: perceptions of career ending." *Journal of Managerial Psychology*, 24(2), 102–17. https://doi.org/10.1108/02683940910928838

Cardoso, A.R., P. Guimarães, and J. Varejão. (2011). "Are older workers worthy of their pay? An empirical investigation of age-productivity and age-wage nexuses." *De Economist*, 159(2), 95–144. https://doi.org/10.1007/s10645-011-9163-8

Chan, W., R.R. Mccrae, F. De Fruyt, L. Jussim, C.E. Löckenhoff, M. De Bolle, and A. Terracciano. (2012). "Stereotypes of age differences in personality traits: Universal and accurate?" *Journal of Personality and Social Psychology*, 103(6), 1050–66. https://doi.org/10.1037/a0029712

Diani, M. (2015). "Social movements, networks and." *The Blackwell Encyclopedia of Sociology*. https://doi.org/10.1002/9781405165518.wbeoss162.pub2

Fisher, G.G., D.S. Chaffee, and A. Sonnega. (2016). "Retirement timing: A review and recommendations for future research." *Work, Aging and Retirement*, 2(2), 230–61. https://doi.org/10.1093/workar/waw001

Graham, I.D., J. Logan, M.B. Harrison, S.E. Straus, J. Tetroe, W. Caswell, and N. Robinson. (2006). "Lost in knowledge translation: Time for a map?" *Journal of Continuing Education in the Health Professions*, 26, 13–24. https://doi.org/10.1002/chp.47

Gratton, L., and A. Scott. (2016). *The 100-year life: Living and working in an age of longevity*. London: Bloomsbury Information.

Henkens, K. (2005). "Stereotyping older workers and retirement: The managers' point of view." *Canadian Journal on Aging*, 24(4), 353–66. https://doi.org/10.1353/cja.2006.0011

James, J.B., S. McKechnie, and J. Swanberg. (2011). "Predicting employee engagement in an age-diverse retail workforce." *Journal of Organizational Behavior*, 32(2), 173–96. https://doi.org/10.1002/job.681

Klassen, D. (2014). "Diversity in Canadian workplaces: Past, present and future." *Career Options*. Retrieved from http://www.careeroptionsmagazine.com/articles/diversity-in-canadian-workplaces-past-present-and-future/ (accessed 21 February 2017).

Munnell, A. (2015). The average retirement age – an update. *The Center for Retirement Research at Boston College*, 15(4), 1–6.

Nickerson, R.S. (1998). "Confirmation bias: A ubiquitous phenomenon in many guises." *Review of General Psychology*, 2(2), 175–220. https://doi.org/10.1037//1089-2680.2.2.175

Pearce, T. (2017). "Do you know how to keep your brain healthy?" *Canadian Living*, 14 February. Retrieved from https://www.canadianliving.com/health/prevention-and-recovery/article/do-you-know-how-to-keep-your-brain-healthy

Peens, M. (2016). *Thriving at work during late career*. Santa Barbara, CA: Fielding Graduate University.

Robertson, A., and C. Tracy. (1998). "Health and productivity of older workers." *Scandinavian Journal of Work, Environment & Health*, 24(2), 85–97. Retrieved from https://doi.org/10.5271/sjweh.284

Smyer, M., and M. Pitt-Catsouphes. (2007). "The meanings of work for older workers." *Generations*, 31(1), 23–30. Retrieved from https://dlib.bc.edu/islandora/object/bc-ir:100731/datastream/PDF/view

Stastista. (2016). "Average life expectancy* in North America for those born in 2015, by gender and region (in years)." Retrieved from https://www.statista.com/statistics/274513/life-expectancy-in-north-america/

Van Dalen, H.P., K. Henkens, and J. Schippers. (2010). "Productivity of older workers: Perceptions of employers and employees." *Population and Development Review*, 36(2), 309–30. https://doi.org/10.1111/j.1728-4457.2010.00331.x

8 From Myth to Smart Strategy

Bersin, J. (2010). "Why talent mobility matters." *Deloitte/Berson* (blog), 19 January. Retrieved from http://blog.bersin.com/why-talent-mobility-matters/

Duggan, M. (2015). "The demographics of social media users." Pew Research Center. Retrieved from http://www.pewinternet.org/2015/08/19/the-demographics-of-social-media-users/

Prensky, M. (2001). "Digital natives, digital immigrants, part 1." *On the Horizon*, 9(5), 1–6. https://doi.org/10.1108/10748120110424816

9 Getting Focused: Tools and Approaches

The Economist. (2009). "Elliott Jaques." *The Economist*, 1 May. Retrieved from http://www.economist.com/node/13599026

Jaques, E. (2017). *Requisite organization: A total system for effective managerial organization and managerial leadership for the 21st century.* London: Routledge.

10 Critical Actions for CEOs

Berger, E.D., and D. Hodgins. (2012). "Age discrimination and paid work." Population Change and Lifecourse Strategic Knowledge Cluster Policy Brief No. 7. Retrieved from http://sociology.uwo.ca/cluster/en/publications/docs/policy_briefs/PolicyBrief7.pdf

Keller, K.L. (2003). *Strategic brand management: Building, measuring, and managing brand equity.* London: Pearson Higher Ed.

Lev, B., and F. Gu. (2016). *The end of accounting and the path forward for investors and managers.* Hoboken, NJ: Wiley.

Vogel, B. (2016). "The end of accounting: Discussion with Professor Baruch Lev." *Discussion & Analysis Magazine*, 36.

11 Critical Actions for HR Leaders

Baker, K., P. Baldwin, K. Donahue, A. Flynn, C. Herbert, and E.L. Jeunesse. (2014). *Housing America's older adults: Meeting the needs of an aging population*. Cambridge, MA: Joint Center for Housing Studies of Harvard University. Retrieved from http://www.jchs.harvard.edu/sites/jchs. harvard.edu/files/jchs-housing_americas_older_adults_2014-ch2.pdf

Bersin, J. (2012). "Big data in HR: Why it's here and what it means." *Deloitte/ Berson* (blog), 17 November. Retrieved from https://blog.bersin.com/ bigdata-in-hr-why-its-here-and-what-it-means/

Bridges, W., and S. Mitchell. (2000). "Leading transition: A new model for change. *Leader to Leader*, 16(3), 30–6.

Goodwin, T. (2015). "The battle is for the customer interface." *Techcrunch*. Retrieved from https://techcrunch.com/2015/03/03/ in-the-age-of-disintermediation-the-battle-is-all-for-the-customer-interface/

Logan, D., J.P. King, and H. Fischer-Wright. (2008). *Tribal leadership: Leveraging natural groups to build a thriving organization*. New York: HarperBusiness.

12 Critical Actions for Frontline Managers

Kunda, Z. (1999). *Social cognition: Making sense of people*. Cambridge, MA: MIT Press.

Receptiviti Inc. (2018). "Receptiviti." Retrieved from https://www.receptiviti. ai/

INDEX

The letter *t* following a page number denotes a table.